The Survival Guide I Wish I Had

BY

TORCHIA JIGGETTS

Dedication

To my readers,

The survival guide is a compelling read for many reasons. My heart leaps with pure joy to know and see that I have overcome so much to become the Woman of God, mother, wife, and friend that I am today. This book is for all who have or may endure the same ordeal as I have. A special dedication to my grandmother, my children, and broken women that are in search for wholeness, my husband, friends, and family. This is a constant reminder that I will leave with you for eternity; keep God first and find peace.

-The world can be dark, but there is light when you're align with the Word of God. Remember to love freely, forgive wholeheartedly, and protect your peace.

Family and friends, I thank you for every seed of encouragement. For those that picked on me, teased me, and counted me out I wholeheartedly forgive you. I thank you because without the humiliation, pain and hurt you all poured into me I would have never known how tough I was while giving my all to be strong in the midst of my brokenness. Overall, I pray for your healing. I pray the Holy Spirit convicts and give you all that Ezekiel 36:26 states. The Lord delivered, healed, leaded, guided, motivated, and restored my strength. You too, should allow God to fight your battles. There is light in obedience. May my words bless you and encourage you along the way. The old things are passed away. It is well!!!

2 Corinthians 5:17, "Therefore if any man be in Christ, he is a new creature: old things are passed away; behold, all things are become new." Jesus said, even if the pain was so intense that we feel we can never forgive a person, we have to forgive them. I, Torchia Chatman-Jiggetts, forgive everyone. I release my first book as an offering to share my story and to help others.

Table of Contents

INTRODUCTION

THE FIRST STEP INTO MY STORY

This is it, my story. It is often said that a writer becomes a writer when words pour out from her soul. It is not a choice, nor a planned decision. It is almost as if the story takes a life of its own, and unravels itself on paper. That was exactly how I became a writer. I never planned it. In fact, the narratives I share through this book are incidents that I had, once upon a time, promised to never disclose to another soul. But, it almost feels destined how one day, I woke up and decided that today, the 18th of December 2020, would be the day I ordered a notebook.

All I can say now is that I think about my life and the stories that surround it a lot. And that I also possess that one eternal belief that every writer seems to share– which is, their experiences are worthy of being read, of being listened to, and of being understood by another person.

As far back as I could remember, I've always loved to write and had invested a lot of time early in my life to read a lot. English was my favorite class in school, even as I wrote poetry, and read a lot of books. Unlike the usual thing's writers would say, the theme of my life has not been the 'typical' kind of life. If you would've told me: one day, I would have a book with my name attached to it, let alone about myself, I would have said you're lying. Me? The nobody that I am?

But, until things in our lives take an unexpected turn, none of us have an idea of the things we are capable of doing because no hourglass tells us what events are about to occur. Yet, they occur.

1

For some, life begins with blunders. These are the people who spend the rest of their lives trying to put things back together and return home to something beautiful and worthy of grace, beauty, and happiness. If they are lucky, they will find peace and healing while they're still alive. If they are not, they will be at peace when their lives come to an end.

I want to state as early as possible in this book that I am one of the fortunate ones who returned home to peace, love, and happiness. And it's all because of God's grace. It's His grace for me. Hallelujah!!

Forgive me if this introduction is not well structured and precise. This is because my life has never been that way. It has been circling between the unshaped, the indeterminate, formless, indefinite, and the unfocused. I was reckless, naïve, daring, and insane. And, while others have taken similar paths without regret, my journey was filled with consequences. And I had to repay the price.

So, the story you're about to read is sparked and driven by my desire for you to read it. It is not about where my life ended or where it all began. It is about me.

I pray I meet you with honesty, the kind of honesty that is enough to tell you how everything is not yet perfect, that life still appears to be scattered even at this very critical moment that I am writing.

I have given a lot of thought to my life. The events in it would play repeatedly and I would just burst into tears. Some nights, I'd pray and then weep so much that it was clear I was at the point of totally breaking down. To get to a place of comfort and mental stability, I had to do something. But, first, I needed to take a break; to share my story with someone other than myself, especially with my children. The last part of sharing my story with them wasn't intentional.

One summer, I got up from a nap to prepare dinner. I must have been overjoyed that day because I remember walking in the front room with a big smile on my face.

"Mommyyyyyyyy," my daughter screamed as soon as she turned and saw me. "What are you doing?" she asked. I smiled back at her, went over to where she was standing, and played with her hair.

"Mommy is going to make dinner."

That evening, I read my scriptures and worked on my book. It had been a long time since I had felt such a joyful and exciting spirit over me. I wanted to share with my kids that I had already gotten up to writing 6 pages. I felt this would be inspiring for them when they become old enough to read it.

"The way you're explaining the details about your book, you can easily make a movie out of it," my son said. Handsome and bright for his age, fifteen, he was standing right behind me, looking at what I was doing. I was sitting on a chair, and I remember turning back to look at him, while smiling. I never told him this, but when I saw my fifteen-year-old son, standing behind me in his 5 feet 9-inch frame and his beautiful head filled with dreadlocks, I was reminded of a guardian angel. Perhaps it was the way the colors played with the room, illuminating his hazel eyes and unspoken wisdom.

His words brought the necessary warmth to my heart.

I had already told them about my granny's role in my life before this.

"I promise you guys that everything I just said is relevant to my granny."

Memory is important to me. I remember things because they help me to understand the fundamentals of my life, the needed reflection of my past, while, at the same time, offering me the possibility to use all my experiences to appreciate who I was and who I am now. Even though there are certain events that I would prefer to forget, I value my memories.

I believe that by writing, I am giving not only to my children but also to someone else in the unknown world outside my own instructions to learn from my mistakes and to remember my courage to live and do better.

Memory is something that the abused would like to forget. Some circumstances are unwelcomed in the act of remembering because they can wreak chaos on our perceptions, emotions, and mental health, and trigger a way to self-destruction. On a closer inspection, however, memory is one of our weapons to do amazing things that we have always been capable of. To remember and accept your journey at each stage of life is a thing of courage. I remember things a lot, which is why I write.

After my son's remark, a fresh wave of memory washed over me for a brief moment. Immediately, I went to tell him how I'd just written about the time granny rescued me. They were listening to everything I was saying until I mentioned that part.

"Mommy, how did big granny rescue you?" my daughter blurted out. She was just eight years old then, not much older than I was when I needed rescuing. Suddenly, I felt petrified because I realized that what had happened to me, could also happen to her. As a mother, I always pride myself in being a mother who supports her children from the sidelines, never imposing her view of the world on them. But now,

I wanted to grab my baby girl and never let her out of sight. I thought about what she asked me, so innocently; *why did I need rescuing?*

The words dried in my mouth at first. It took a few seconds to quickly process what I was going to tell her before I finally turned and looked at her. During my transformation, I've learned that holding back something that can be educational, and life-changing is not the right thing to do. I wanted my children to know my story— the failures in it, the victories in it, and how I got to where I am today. Most importantly, I wanted to make sure that my children did not go through life feeling alone and afraid of coming to me for help when they most needed. As a child, no one had talked to me about the bad things that can happen to children, so when it happened to me, I thought I had to face them alone. As a mother, that was not what I wanted for my kids, especially my daughter. I wanted her to walk through life with her eyes wide open, and to know that no matter what happened, mommy would always be here to help her through her journey, and whatever challenges the journey may bring with them.

I told my children to sit down. When they did, I began to narrate to them how my mother's "boyfriend" abused me, and other horrible things he did to me. Since this was a very sensitive matter to discuss with them at that age, I felt it was the best thing to do. There was never a right age for talks like this. The earlier they understood, the better it would be for our mother-child relationship.

Talking to my children about my past reawakened horrifying memories that I had assumed had been buried with my past. I was mistaken. I felt like my eyes had formed a pool of tears on the floor. I mentioned earlier that memory is important, no matter how hard we have tried to deny it. Talking to my children helped me see and appreciate my life in ways I'd never done before. It projected my courage to me and when I was coming to the end of our discussion, I saw the look in their eyes and how attentive they'd been all along, I immediately realized how grateful it is to have my children listen to the story of my life and not judge me. I was relieved.

I told my children that if Granny hadn't intervened and told Joe, my mother's boyfriend, to stop sexually molesting her granddaughter, I would have never known what could have happened to me later.

If she was alive today, I would love to ask her what prompted her to do what she did, and what made her come to my aid that day. Thinking about this, I told my children that as part of the larger human family, we must all learn to cherish each other and be ready to be there when we are needed. It's difficult to imagine how my life would have turned out today had my Granny not showed up for me.

That day, I cried a lot while telling my story. But I made it clear to them that my tears were not the result of sadness. They were tears of joy and gratitude that I had survived the rain.

I hope that my story will inspire, encourage, and motivate you. I want to show you that your life has value and that there is room for forgiveness, personal growth, well-being, and an unwavering sense of purpose.

I understand that we all have differences, and that life affects us in many ways. But this is a book that tells the whole story. I want to talk to you about some very explicit topics that most people who have had similar experiences like me would be too ashamed to share. The things that happened to me are things I want the world to know. They are not things I desire to take to the grave with me due to embarrassment and shame. Among the many lessons, I've learned from my relationship with God is to be unafraid of the truth, no matter how ugly and bitter it appears in the eyes and tastes in the mouth. I owe the universe nothing but the truth.

And, even at this stage of this book, this is something I would also love to advise you to do. Do not be ashamed of your experiences. It is your life, not the lives of others. Sometimes, what lies behind the masks on our faces is something that shows how important, resilient, kind, and adequate we are. Regardless of our heinous and traumatic experiences, these are the sides of ourselves that we should never be afraid to show the world. God has promised to be with us every step of the way, even when we don't deserve it. I am a living witness.

I may not know you, but I care about you. So, I humbly invite you to join me on this ride. You may get bored. You may cry, but I can assure you that my bumps in the road will fill you up inside.

Each day, I learn something new about my life and how its many pieces are still scattered. I haven't figured everything out yet. But by writing this book (and hopefully not the last one), I am attempting to draw attention to the puzzles and place them back where they belong.

I'll say it again: memory is important to me. If I hadn't started writing this book, I wouldn't be able to remember any of the things I'm going to say here, let alone everything that happened to that young, vulnerable girl I used to be. Even though I wished I had the survival guide I have access to today, I am happy to inform you that I am living my life with no regrets. I've been seeing a therapist since 2018, and I am still exploring all of my options for healing.

While writing this book and experiencing everything in it for myself, I imagined myself in the position of the reader and I wondered: Do we have moments of intercession where readers can go get some refreshments like they do at plays? If this is so, I recommend that you, my dearest reader, get a snack because everything that happened before my life turned for the better was just so dirty, really dirty, and filthy. And, yes, quite embarrassing, too.

And I am going to tell everything.

Lord help me.

CHAPTER 1

EVERYONE BREAKS

"The world breaks everyone, and afterward, many are strong at the broken places." — Ernest Hemingway

The South Side is the largest of the three sides of Chicago, the third-largest city in the United States of America, and is divided by the Chicago River and its various branches. This is the place where I was born. I could have added that it was also here that I met and became friends with people of various ethnicities, a fact that the city is well known for. But I'm afraid I can't. Because, as far as I could recall, the only thing I knew about Chicago was that it was where I was born. I don't know anything about its living conditions, neighborhoods, or cultural and social offerings.

I often hid my origins due to a combination of circumstances, particularly my stereotypical nature and associations. I've heard that a lot of people do this. They feel less loyal to their birthplace as a result of the act, as well as the need to acknowledge it. However, I was not ashamed of my hometown, nor was I attempting to distance myself from its "culture." All I felt was that, I was one of those who felt excluded as if they were missing out on something. Chicago's blood simply does not run through me, and as a result, my pride in it has been diminished. Unfortunately for me, this would set the course of my life in motion. I would spend several years, especially with my son, moving from city to city, looking for a place to call home.

My mother's fear of raising my siblings and me in an environment where she had spent the majority of her life with her seven brothers and sisters was the reason for my early departure from the South Side. Whatever her reasons for leaving, it's possible she wanted to keep us from having the same terrible experiences she had while living there, or she wanted us to grow up somewhere where we could have better educational and other life opportunities. Also, I'd like to believe that the high crime rate in Chicago contributed to her decision to leave the city permanently.

I grew up with two older brothers and a younger sister. We shared the same father, which was unusual even for an African-American family.

Sadly, there was nowhere that I could actually call home. My mother was a single mother who raised me and my siblings all by herself. My father abandoned her when I was two years old. I'd never met him or known anything about his relationship with my mother.

I used to wonder what kind of man my father was and how my life would have turned out differently if he had been with us. Had he ever thought about me if he was somewhere? What can he say about us? Did he have any idea we existed? I imagined him to be somewhere out there, and the thought made me nervous. Although it was a thought I couldn't shake, as it kept occupying my mind now and then, I knew I had to make a decision, early in life: keep thinking about my father or simply leave things the way I met them and move on with my life.

After my father departed, my mother gathered us, bundled everything, and moved us to Minnesota, where we began a new life.

We grew up as children without a father in the home, in poverty, shifting our bodies from one shelter to the next.

As time went on, I began to piece together the drama and dirt that made my father and mother separate.

My father had cheated on her with two different women and had a child with each of them. When my mother was pregnant with my younger sister, one of the women my father was cheating with was also pregnant for him. It didn't take long for my mother to find out. Prompted by the scorn and anger, she packed her things and left for Minnesota.

In Minnesota, we lived on the second floor of a 4-plex apartment building while my Granny was downstairs. At the time, my uncle had been living with her for some years. The eyes of a child looked at everyone from the place of innocence. If I'd known even at that age that this nice-looking young man would be the same monster that would ruin my life for a very long time, I would have taken the necessary steps to avoid that. But I was a child, and, like all children, I was at his mercy. I realize that for most survivors of sexual abuse, merely acknowledging that they have been abused could be devastating for them and their families, especially if the abuser belongs to the same family. It is not uncommon for victims to come forward several years later to admit that they were abused. Whether this delay was done out of the need not to destroy a family relationship or the victim wanted to attain a certain period of maturity before they could be able to handle the trauma, I can't say. It was different in my case. I believe I kept mine to myself to cover the scars and the expected disbelief from family members.

"You want some candy?" my uncle asked me. He'd begun to come up to our house through the back door whenever he noticed there weren't many people in the house.

"Yes!!!" I'd answer excitedly.

"I got some candy."

"You do?"

"Of course, I do. You come downstairs with me, and I'll give you some. Deal?" he asked, looking at me in the eyes, persuasively.

Downstairs.

My uncle was holding a glass of gin as he walked behind me. Right now, thinking about this, I could feel his eyes on me as I walked. Once we were in the room, everywhere was quiet. No one was in the house, except the giant photo of my granny on the wall, watching as my uncle handed me candy. "Here, you take a bite."

I did.

"I see you like it," he said, smiling at me.

I took another bite before I answered him. "I do, uncle."

"I know, right," he said, and pulled me closer to him. "Now, there's more where that came from."

"Really?" I was excited.

"As far as we are both know from today, I am your candy man."

As he spoke, I felt a slight pressure behind me. It was my uncle's hand running through the fabrics of my backsides. I turned to see him smiling at me.

"Hey, don't worry. I'm right here with you. Don't be afraid. I'm just checking to make sure you're nice and clean."

At that age, it was hard for me to know the weight of those words.

I stood there, momentarily taking bites of my candy, as he pulled my pants down.

"Lean over," he said, in a very gentle voice.

I did.

He took his time as he touched me gently, rubbing his hands all over my back, touching me in places and in a way that no uncle should ever touch his niece, especially one as young as I was all those years ago. His breath, getting heavy and deeper, pored into my skin.

After what seemed like an eternity, I felt his breath move away from my body.

"We're done. You're a clean girl, you know that, don't you?"

"Yes, uncle."

"Good. Now," he continued, bringing his face closer to look deeply into my eyes. "This is our little secret. And we're just having fun. And the more it happens, the more candy you get to have."

That was the first day. And it didn't stop there. Each day that he and I met, the candy increased. And with that, he grew bolder. I still couldn't figure out the meaning of everything he was doing to me. Between the ages of 13-15, I was around my uncle a lot. Neither my mom nor my granny suspected what was going on between us. I loved to think that they accepted his fondness of me and its accompanying generosity as a mark of his blood relations with me. Besides, he was well-known around the neighborhood as a very nice man.

Whenever he came to our house with his girlfriend, he would never leave without giving me shoes, money, or even asking me to go to the movies with them. I loved the fact that he would always do this for me and take me to the movies. It took me years later to understand that his motives for being so close to me all the time was to damage and control me.

He was afraid of my memories. He didn't want me to suddenly remember certain things someday and divulge all the things he had been doing to me. He was maintaining proximity so he could create contradictory scenarios and make me out to be the liar when the occasion demanded to be aired out. He was a manipulator from the start who had planned his moves carefully to avoid complications.

In retrospect, he exhibited all the signs of emotional and psychological abuse. By being so involved in my life, he absolved himself of sin. Everyone around me thought he was a caring, doting uncle; the very image he wanted to portray. He bombarded me with affection and love, like any uncle would, hoping that in the future, I would try to fight my own mind. He tried to gaslight me against my own memories and knew that by behaving the way he did, I would end up believing that my memories were nothing but imagination. After all, he treated me so well with the gifts. He wanted me to know that someone that kind could never have been as cruel as I might one day remember him to be.

When you look around you, you would see that it seems as if evil people continuously get away with their evil actions that have caused ruins and damage to many. But whatever way you look at it, this does not mean that they truly get away with it forever. Or that such actions, mostly done in secret, would not see the light of the day someday. I am a believer that what we reap what we sow. This was what happened to my uncle.

In 2009, when I was about 21, we were all at Granny's house when one of my brothers and a few others present began a conversation that later covered the statutes of limitations. I wasn't fully following their conversation as I was engaged in other small talks with other family members.

Suddenly, they began to discuss my uncle and all the wrong doings he had done. I was drawn away by the mention of his name.

By then, even the thought of him would send a shiver down my spine. It was almost as though I could never shed his skin off me. At that moment, I wondered if it was the right time to finally say something since, I was one of the major people that he had carried out his wrong doings upon. Instead, the more I listened to their talks, the more I realized that they were just gossip talks that offered no healing but added bruises to my pain. There was no sympathy, and no reassurance that his victims, who shared the same blood with him, would be fine. I chose to stay quiet and sat back while the rest talked about it. I felt a deep pain for the victims they were speaking of. I wanted to jump to their defense, to my defense. But, I didn't. Why? I don't know. I guess it's because I was in shock and trying to keep it together. A conversation like that can be very triggering, and I was trying to control myself from flying off the rail. I hoped that I was the only woman at that table who understood what it meant to survive my uncle's assaults. But I stayed silent. I wondered, were there other silent victims at that table?

Two days later, while my mother and I were together alone in the evening, she looked at me. I knew she had something to say.

"What is it, momma?" I asked. She smiled sadly.

"I didn't know what to do when they told me what he did to you?" she confessed. I had no words to say. Instead, I took my eyes away from her. "I didn't know how to handle the situation."

I was thinking of the best way to respond to her when she asked the question that I dreaded the most, one that I heard several times from the mouths of people who could offer no healing or respite to me.

"How come you kept this a secret, and have managed to hide it for so long?"

Even though I found her question irritating, it took all of my restraint not to lash out at her when she went on:

"Things like this would be overlooked as people would have said there's no way you could have remembered that from a young age."

I didn't know why she said that, or could it be that it was the best she could do to handle that situation. How could anyone believe that children between the ages of 5-7 could not, much later in life, remember and retain the events that happened to them during those years?

After that conversation with my mother, I wanted nothing to do with the people around me. Neither did I want to give anyone an explanation for the things that happened to me when I was a kid. I was also not looking forward to apologies– the innumerable "sorrys" that were likely to come from people.

However, even as this was going on, my life kept taking up different shapes. We were moving a lot, and within each city, everything that was supposed to have made meaning for me became nothing but darkness.

I wasn't prepared for it.

CHAPTER 2

THE OUTSIDER

"Where you come from is gone, where you thought you were going to was never there... In yourself right now is all the place you've got."

— Flannery O'Connor, *Wise Blood*

For my mother, the idea of a better opportunity for us was moving to one of the predominantly "white" and richest cities – Edina. The first-rig suburb in Minneapolis that began to taste prosperity as a farming and milling community in the 19th Century, Edina is notorious for its actions to keep the city completely, conservative, white and wealthy. This was the place my mother moved us to.

Growing up as a child, I was sightless to color. I had no idea what the color of my skin meant to the most conservative white man. All I was grateful for was that I was alive, black, and again alive. I was a child. And all I needed to do was what a child does– move in between my world without giving thoughts to racism, minority, and majority. These were ideas that were alien to me.

During those days, I'd say including myself, and this is an estimate, there were maybe 5 other minority "Black students" in the 6th/7th grade total. I'm glad the middle schools out there went to 9th grade, otherwise I would not have discovered all that I have discovered so far.

I need you to understand that what I just said was not my way of labeling things. It was society's way. I just needed to make that clear before my story continues.

When I grew up, I saw no color. I only saw the odds of color. Although my mother endured some tough things as an adult, and I witnessed some of them myself, I appreciate and love her so much more because she raised us in the image of God.

I am thankful for my mother, and I am glad that I never gave up on her, rather I understood her. I never could understand how or why I could feel others' pain and suffering as if I saw through them and into their hollow souls. Like what was going on outwardly I did not see.

Shortly after we moved from the "suburbs" and then thrown into one of the most proclaimed dangerous cities, North Minneapolis. That would not have affected me later on, right? As soon as we arrived, it didn't take long for those around to begin teasing me for the way I talked.

"You act white, and you talk too proper," they'd say to me. I would get teased all of the time. I did not have friends; it was the other way round. People dumped on me and used me as their disposable and usable toy to shame and then throw away.

To me, throughout my life, I thought I had befriended people, but little did I know to them I was not their friend. I was the "nobody" in the neighborhood. The derisive name-callings and tags had pushed me to the wall on many occasions.

We were living in Hopkins during my Edina school days, and I remember that my mother had been kicked out of our apartment and ended up having to move into a shabby shelter.

During that time, she left me to reside with a classmate of mine from Edina middle school, who was living in the same apartment complex. I am not sure how that agreement came about between her and the mother, but I will say my friend's mother was so kind, humble, nice, warm, caring, generous, and nurturing. These were qualities I hadn't felt from anyone before until then. And for her to have taken me in without knowing me like that, only proved that she and her daughters were really good people.

My classmate had an opposing twin sister. And if you are wondering, the clarification is concrete. Not all twins are close and friendly. They were total opposites, yet the love was still there without a doubt. I felt like they were the modern-day Mary Kate and Ashley.

Together, we would watch a lot of movies after which we would settle in for the night. Each night, I would stay awake in bed, wondering: Why did my mom leave me?

At that specified time I wish I knew. I was desperately missing her.

Once, I entered a talent show with five other girls, we made up a dance to Christina Aguilera's "What A Girl Wants."

We did an outstanding job, and to a standing ovation. Later, I came to realization that my mom managed to find a way to attend to see me dance, after months since I last saw her.

One morning, I stepped into the living room, and on a table close to the wall, I found the last known phone number for my mother. I had the thought of giving her a call. The next day, it was sunny outside, I was at school, and I asked the lady at the front desk in the office if I could call my mom. The phone rang about three times, although it seemed to me to be ringing forever. I sighed and was about to give up when I heard her voice. She had finally answered!

Writing this today, I cannot remember what exactly it was that we discussed. But I remember my outcry that critical day:

"Mom, when are you coming to get me?"

I was 12 years old at the time.

"I'm working, baby. I'm working on that. I'm going to see you soon."

After hearing that my heart dropped, like a mango fruit, on the inside and I could feel the water set in my eyes. I was overwhelmed by distress, abandonment, pain, and hurt. My tears were saltier than the water of the oceans. Before the call ended, I rushed back to reality:

"I love you, mom," I said softly.

Her voice returned to me with the same words, and even more, emotions attached to it.

"I love you too Torchia."

I remember wanting to be glued to my mother when I was a little girl. I didn't have any acquaintances. I went to parks and played with toys, but my favorite part was watching my mother step. She was a big fan of oldies. She was a huge fan of Whitney Houston.

I continued to live with my new family. I was introduced to God while living with them. I later learned a little bit about Him. They went to church, bible study, and frequently took us on retreats. In addition, I participated in a church play with the girls. I have to be completely honest with you here. I hadn't given it much thought until now when I realized that maybe, the Lord was watching over me during this time and I was oblivious to it.

A lot of time passed after that phone call before I ended up getting reunited with my mom.

I love her. It's always an honor and a light of gratitude to have my lovely mother by my side and rocking with me. I Just wanted to preface and re-iterate this. I became really ill. Too sick to the extent that I almost died. I could not move, my body ached. One day, I overheard Ms. Katy, the twins' mom, talking on the phone with my mother in a pleasant, calm, yet stern voice.

"You need to come pick your daughter up and take her to the hospital," she said with distress in her voice. You need to see her with your eyes. She is laying here, completely unable to move."

There was silence. And then Ms. Katy's voice resumed.

It was threatening.

"I will call child protection service if you don't show up." They exchanged a few more words before the call ended.

Ms. Katy did not have any of my medical or personal information. Clearly, at the time, I did not understand what any of the verbiage she was speaking meant. She always made me feel a part of the family just as if I were her real daughter and as if her girls, Jes and Jessy, were my real sisters.

I will say one of the most exciting and memorable moments I shared with them as we got to drive a car for the first time. Ms. Katy had purchased a red convertible BMW. She had taken us to a beautiful place to drive along a dirt road and we all got to drive a mile each. One may say how is this child still functioning after all of this trauma? I am still searching for that answer myself.

CHAPTER 3

DARKNESS LOOMING

"The darker the night, the brighter the stars,
The deeper the grief, the closer is God!"
— Fyodor Dostoevsky, Crime and Punishment

At last, my mother came for me. I noticed that she had been staying at a local shelter. Later on, during my adult years, my mother confessed to me that it had been easier for her to have one child with her.

Here, I am taking a journey backward, right to those disgusting moments in my childhood again.

Before we moved to Edina, we resided in Minneapolis until I was in 4th grade.

It is during this very moment I just realized that between the ages of five and ten, I experienced things that a young, innocent, and pure little girl should not have had encountered.

There was a guy that my mother began dating while living in Chicago, before moving to Minneapolis. He followed my mother. They dated for years until I was about seven and a half years old. He was like our first father figure. Well, at least for my sister and me. My brothers were old enough to have been around our biological father.

My mom's new man was so kind. Very often, he would take my sister and me to the park, malls, and then several other places to eat. He even went as far as helping us with school work, and so much more. After he and my mother stopped dating– I never was told why they stopped dating, but I sure wished they hadn't– he remained in our lives. He would keep us during the weekends and just care for us with no hesitation. He stayed in our lives as much as he could until my mother began dating a new guy, who ended up becoming our abuser over the next 2 to 3 years. His name was Joe. And when I met him, it marked the turning point in my life where the darkness first began to come for me.

You'd always find Joe wearing a Jerry curl, and driving a decked-out Cadillac. Outwardly he appeared quite charming to other adults, but it's like I always could see right through him.

He had a way with words. Joe treated my sister and me like animals and slaves and scum of the earth. We could not talk. A lot of his abuse would occur while my mother was at work and some of the times when she was home and unaware. When doing chores, we had to get on our hands and knees and scrub for hours. When we ate our meals, he sat in the kitchen and watched us, and would not let us get up until we were finished.

One day, it struck me, when he had given us cereal with milk that was frozen, and it turned our cereal into a soggy chunky inedible thing. However, he forced the cereal down our throats. We would be choking on our food and crying all at the same time. If we ever asked a question about anything, I mean anything, he would tell us to shut up and not to speak. He would make us stand against the wall in a squat position for hours, and then barked at us.

"If you move an inch before I get back here, I will beat you!"

That had a drastic and negative effect on me even today. As an adult, I do not like to do body-turning exercises. They give the nostalgia of a harsh past.

Joe always had a wooden paddle in his hand to beat us with it. He never laid his hands on or abused my brothers though. I remember one day I had built the courage to stand up to him and yelled at him.

"Leave us alone, you dummy!" I can't remember the exact wording, but I guess that was the wrong thing to do as he charged into our room and began punching me. All I knew to do was to kick and scream at him.

"Get off of me!"

A few days after that altercation, I told myself that I was leaving. I had no idea where I would go. All I know was that I was going to run away. The Lion King was the newest movie out around that time. I referenced the movie because I had an orange duffle bag with the characters on it. I had gotten it from one of the free stores that I went to with my mom one day where the items there were free or donated. That's where we got all of our clothing we wore from.

I filled my clothes up into that bag and proceeded out of the house. My older cousins and a few other family members were there sitting on the porch at the time. We lived across the street from a large parking lot. I began to walk. I could hear everyone laughing and talking about me.

"Girl where do you think you are going with your tiny bag?" One of them asked, laughing.

I didn't even turn around.

"I am running away!" I remember saying.

I got three blocks down the road and looked back, and no one had come after me. I walked an additional block and then turned back around, heading back home, into my room. That afternoon, I cried and cried until I fell asleep. That sleep took nothing out of the more darkness that would still come my way.

In 4th grade, I experienced a moment of what felt like excitement and happiness. Elementary school is not the same as back in the day.

In elementary school, we used to be given a list of field trip options that were available for all students, school-wide. The choices ranged from Roller gardens, Zoo, Park, Movies, and so on. I made Roller gardens my choice. It just felt like a chance to detach from what I was going through at home so that I could feel normal and somewhat relieved. I was so excited that I picked out my clothes the night before. I even ironed and put creases in my pants. It was a great thing back in the day.

The next morning, I had gotten up early because the excitement was real. I got dressed and turned the television on and sat on the bed until it was time to go to my bus stop. Since I was ready so early, I thought I might as well take my time going to the bus stop. Within 5-10 minutes, my world shattered. Joe decided to wake up on the wrong side of the bed.

"Why haven't you left for your bus stop yet?" he asked as soon as he stepped into my room.

I explained things to him. I delayed because I was already dressed to go and wanted to rest a little while.

"Granny would walk me," I said.

A smile crossed his face, almost wickedly. He must've liked that. Or maybe my tone hurt him. I didn't know who the devil was, but his whole person changed, and anger and rage appeared abruptly for no apparent reasons. All I did was to be patiently sitting, waiting for the next thunderbolt.

"You are getting out of here right now," he shouted.

"I don't want to leave yet it's still early," I replied, with a raised pitch.

We lived in a three-story house at the time and the bedrooms were on the second floor. Joe began to drag me down two flights of stairs until I was out of the house. I was kicking and screaming for him to stop but he wouldn't. I could not get out of his bone-breaking hold as he also had me by the neck. I was darn well convinced that the neighbors and everyone who was outside heard and saw what was going on. No one did or said anything. Joe literally dragged me farther, two blocks down the street. We made it to my bus stop and there I was, face full of tears, and snot. This man still had me by the neck. He was really about to send me on the bus in poor condition: ripped and dirty clothing. And then I heard a voice behind us, one that I recognized very well.

My Granny.

I could see her running towards us and once she got to the bus stop, she screamed at him.

"Joe, let her go. Come on now, Joe. Let my granddaughter go. Give her to me."

He respected my granny and let me free. I wonder if he had realized or knew anyone was awake or didn't care either way. My granny held me in her arms as we walked back to the house. She helped me wash up and changed clothes and walked me to school. It was a long and uneasy walk, but it allowed me to recollect my thoughts and build motivation. That day was quite heavy and intense to my soul, but I knew that the field trip was the only fun thing I had, and now that I think about it, I'd say it was more of an escape.

May the Lord, the God that I serve, rest my Granny's loving soul. She had suffered a stroke in April 2019, and then finally passed away in February 2020. At one point, it appeared as if her recovery was going well until it went downhill towards the holiday season. The last time I saw her was Christmas. I will always be eternally thankful to have shared some of her final moments in peace and harmony alongside family. I remember always spending time at her house. I remember being with her all summer, she had gotten me so attached to watching *Soap Operas* and *The Young and the Restless*. I remember enjoying and spending precious time with her. She and I hit a rough patch but as I've reflected, it was due to my juvenile antics and understanding.

I was pregnant with my daughter at the time, and I was temporarily without a place to stay. I was around 24 years old then. At the time, my younger cousin lived there as my granny adopted her when she was younger. My cousin and I had gotten into an altercation. Pregnancy hormones along with other things took over, and I was told to leave by the end of the week. I didn't blame my granny for this. Instead, I didn't fully appreciate her generosity to give up her space to assist me during that time. A year or two later, I managed to reconnect with her, and it was so amazing. She went on to state the exact month and day she had last seen me and how she enjoyed me, and I started crying. I was blessed to have re-established a positive and healthy relationship with her before her passing.

Here, again, I take another step back into my life before Edina.

After 4th grade, we had to move out of our home. This is one of the positive memories I have:

My mother, all-smiling, is opening her door and welcoming everyone: family, friends. Everyone. She also allowed adult cousins to live with us for extended periods. However, with the constant physical abuse going on, I never got to enjoy living in that house. I remember being worried about my mother's life while living there. She had become severely ill with pneumonia. She would have to use a ventilator to help her breathe, but all she did was persevere. I was young and all I could do was just watch and feel helpless.

How many of you have ever felt helpless in a situation? I'd say we all have. However, those who live with pride would act as if their lives do not bring problems.

We later went on to live in, yet another shelter called Sharing and Caring, and this was all because the owner of the house sold it and did not tell my mother until 30 days before closing.

CHAPTER 4

DARKNESS

"But I know, somehow, that only when it is dark enough can you see the stars" — Martin Luther King, Jr.

Selling our family home was nothing but a pretty darn inconsiderate thing to do. Sharing and Caring was a very nice shelter, considering the prior ones we resided in that offered a room with a bathroom, and two beds for a family of five to sleep in. It was like a studio apartment that had one room and nicely designed bunk beds that were roomy—one for each of us to lay on and not have to share.

We stayed there for a good six months and shortly after that, we made our move to Edina. Elementary schools out there appeared to be more structured and in order. The teaching materials and curriculum were challenging and were not the same as in the "city of Minneapolis" schools. 5th grade was alright. My Teacher Ms. M was so nice, soft, and helpful in a manner that screamed: "Yessss! That's what teachers are supposed to be." However, I haven't experienced that type of kindness anywhere else. She was left-handed. I remember when we had free time, I would try writing on the whiteboard using my left hand. I continued practicing it, for sure, I would have been ambidextrous. Kids out there had boyfriends and girlfriends, but not in the context you think. They were able to go to each other's houses to hang out, watch movies, play games, and sports, go to games and events. But in the city, their version of boyfriend and girlfriend meant something physical and adultlike behavior. I wish we never moved to the city.

I was that kid that many would call naive, but I wasn't. My mother didn't talk to my sister and me about boys. I was never taught about sex. My mother never published any adult type of things around us which I am thankful for because why should children see things that may alter or hinder their lives?

But I did have what others may call a crush, although I saw him as a really nice friend. His name was Stan. He was blond-haired, freckle-faced, with bright blue eyes. He was considered a popular kid. The cool part was that his mother volunteered for our classroom each week during the reading group. A group of us would hang out at his house to a point that Stan's mother knew who we all were. She would make us snacks while we hung around their pool and basketball court. Their house was like a mansion.

I would like to intercede here; to share that it's been roughly over two weeks since I've written. I had to pause and reset because I realized I was trying to get you to like me by altering or adding sarcasm or alluring phrases where they weren't needed. Like here, I was downplaying myself to please an audience that I don't even know. But as my therapist says:

The effects of trauma and your subconscious would cause you to do whatever you can to be a "Factor to others" but not a factor to yourself.

I have discovered at the amazing age of 33 that being myself no matter what is important. This is not a false story. This is my real-life testimony. Things will be revealed that I am not proud of. And to keep it 100% real, some of the encounters I have had should have left me dead. I shouldn't be alive, but God kept me. Do you hear what I just said? GOD KEPT ME!!! I ask that you guys bear with me as I continue pouring out my test and trials of life to you until the receptacle is empty.

My history, with all its joys and sorrows, goes on before you, again. Indulge me with kindness.

6th grade was better than 5th because more students shared my same skin tone. Other minorities were present, too. It was pretty hard to fit in and I was bullied by this girl in my class nonstop. People seemed to have the gravitas to me because I was shy, lowly, meek, quiet, and calm, and maybe didn't "act like" the black people that were portrayed in the entertainment world or "City" area.

Maybe it was that she knew how greatly amazing I was that she picked on me to crush my spirit and make me feel worthless. Kids wore brands like Abercrombie and Fitch. Old Navy, American Eagle. You can catch the drift, meanwhile, I love my mother because I wasn't brought up on labels and name brands. I would wear clothing that was from Kmart. I remember signing up for classes such as the band to try to portray as if I had talents. I played the flute, but still got teased. By the end of the school year, I'd say that I sprouted out of my shell and ended up befriending a nice group of girls.

I had mentioned earlier about dancing to Christina Aguilera's "What A Girl Wants" and that the standing ovation was magical. That had to be one of the positive highlights of my youth life in Edina. Well, that and meeting who I called my childhood best friend, Deidra.

Deidra M. loved Eminem. Rap was her thing, and you could not tell her otherwise. Funnily, her brother liked rock. She loved some Mountain Dew.

I loved her family, especially her mom. How I loved her mother! She made the most beautiful jewelry. Such a warm, nurturing, helpful, understanding woman and easy to talk to. Her Father was cool, too! He was bedridden, direct, yet open-minded. Despite what I was going through personally, they still treated me like a person of worth.

Deidra and I tried our best to keep in touch with each other. She and I connected for a short, yet valuable time during high school. I remember sharing with her that I had a son. He must have been around 6 months then. She and I wanted to see each other, and no questions came from her mother. She even instructed me to come along with my son's playpen. While there, her mother offered to watch him so that we could go to Southdale Mall. Deidra had her license. I promise you guys, even as I write this, I see God's hand all over my life, protecting me by showing me love through others to provide me with hope.

Lord knows I wish we hadn't left the shelter we were staying in. We lived there for almost a year. For the first few months of 7th grade that we lived there, everyone somehow knew which school bus transported the shelter kids which caused embarrassment. Kids that travel by bus were considered lowly.

My hands are shaking right now remembering this, and I feel my blood pressure rising at this very moment along with the piercing feeling in the pit of my stomach. The next set of events I thought were only going to the grave with me. But because I see now and God has allowed me to see today, it's a part of my purpose to show all of my scars and carry my cross in front of the world. I feel that attachment issues may be a trend also that I discovered.

The crazy part is the school I attended during elementary school was where I spent the rest of my middle school days. I never shared with my mother the bullying, name-calling, frustrations, physical attacks by other students that occurred while attending that school and must have thought that by placing us back into the school that we were already accustomed to.

Those who knew me hadn't seen my face since 4th grade and here I magically re-appeared.

"Oh, she left for the suburbs, but we saw her come right back to where the real deal was."

That was one of many comments I received. It wasn't welcoming from most, but from others and new students who didn't know of me were welcoming.

Andersen was a huge school. It went from grades Pre-K to 8th grade, however, initially went up to 12th grade. At one point my two brothers and I attended at the same time.

A very fond memory that came to my mind during kindergarten before my innocence was taken, during free play time, I wouldn't go play with dolls or other girly things; although I played with dolls, my interest turned only when a few of us were present. I would play with the same kids every day at the cassette tape play station and we would listen to this one song. At that time, I was not sure why it gravitated to me; now I do. The song was Michael Bolton's "Lean on Me" and I still clearly remember some of the lyrics:

Lean on me,
When you're not strong
And I'll be your friend
I'll help you carry on
For it won't be long, till I'm gonna need
Somebody to lean on

I'd say from K-2, the school was good. My mother must have been making a pretty decent living. She dressed us up well. Coming to school with our hair done every day. School pictures catalog were perfect. I had long flowy hair. I got "noticed" by students until Grades 3-4 where my life became more challenging.

I'd developed a mole that seemed to have appeared overnight and outgrown a piece of my skin, poking out. I was unhappy. Here's one more thing to be teased and humiliated for. I went to school wearing clothes from the free store. My appearance was visibly changing, and I believed my classmates could start seeing my struggle through that. My hair wasn't getting done anymore.

One morning, one of my brothers combed and brushed my hair for me, and placed a ponytail in my head.

"Girl, you didn't know how to put a ponytail in your head or comb your hair?" I was teased.

"No, I do not. Sorry."

My hair started falling out and by the end of 4th grade I barely had anything left. The 4th and 5th-grade pictures would make you cringe. Even my yearbook archives were rough, but that didn't affect me during those days. I continued to walk and keep everything inside and would still treat those who bullied me nicely.

During recess one day, a boy from my class, the class clown, someone who knew the school principal quite well. He approached me and just started calling me so many names and curse words which then I didn't know were curse words. He was pushing and kicking me for no reason. I started shaking, tears were flowing down my eyes, even as the whole class was watching this all take place, nobody said anything.

I remember I kept yelling and screaming, "Leave me alone, leave me alone", but he wouldn't stop. Where did I find the strength to punch him in the nose and make it bleed? I do not know. But I did. Not sure where the teachers were when this kid was attacking me, but I guess when bloodshed was involved, they must have found it important enough. I ended up getting suspended for 3 days, even though I was the traumatized one. That wasn't all. I earned another badge from the bullies to pick on me more. I would be called cha cha cha Chia or Tortilla Chips.

At home, I ended up getting punished for it. Never was I sat down nor asked what happened or was I okay. Nothing like that was spoken in that household during those times. Considering the high level of abuse, having to be in that house around Joe for three days was torture.

One thing positive I can say about that devilish man is that I learned cleanliness. This was a reason why clutter and filth get to me. I found myself as an adult disposing things easier to ensure clean space. I never really cared about having things because of the humble beginning I had.

We moved to North Minneapolis, where things took a turn. There, I learned about sex, rape, STDs, and drinking.

The summer before 8th grade was when guys on our block started to notice me. We had lived there for about a year beforehand and this didn't happen. So, why were they noticing me now? I didn't know.

My mother, brothers, or relatives never talked to me about sexuality. I didn't have friends who knew about it. Heck! I didn't have friends at all. I was always alone. In the house. My sister and I were never really close. Not sure why. And what's strange was my mother never enrolled us in the same schools. She placed us in separate schools all the time. I am not going to even ask my mother why because she has endured enough. This was also the exact time that the darkness became complete. The devil began to have his way and devour my purity.

There was a boy who lived next door to us. He was about 16 or 17.

And he would stop by on days that I would sit on the porch to say hello and he would ask how I was doing. Small talks, nothing that would scream or warn me to say, "Oh he's about to do this to you so back up!"

But after a few weeks went by, he came over one day, as usual, to say hello and make small talk but this specific day was a bit different. He was almost a bit pushy or persistent.

"You ever had sex before?" he asked, becoming bold with me.

"Sex?" I asked.

He nodded like an excited lizard.

I have never been someone who assumes– however, right now, I am assuming that you guys are saying it– she knew dang well what that was.

The world loves to label and associate our living conditions with other things.

"No, I haven't," I said, looking up to him.

"Can I come in so I can show you what it is?" he asked.

To the kid I was back then, everything was harmless.

"Okay," I replied.

My mother wasn't home. It was just my sister and me. I was not sure where my brothers were. We went into the bedroom, and I asked him whatever he was about to show me would it hurt.

"No."

He pulled my blue plaid shorts down and asked me to lay on my back. He began to do whatever he was doing. I must have been too tense or something not to feel anything as I still had no clue what type of activity was happening. I know many kids would defend their parents from this point now; as you all may be tempted to say, "Where was her mother?" Well, she was at work. Keeping a roof over our heads as she refused to let us see another shelter again. And we did not. We were sheltered by my mother which I am thankful for.

He had sex with me two more times after that which the third encounter had gotten scary and I wished I had my mother, brother, or somebody there to help. He had asked me to come to his house this time. It was nighttime too, which was different. I said, okay. I thought we were there alone, but we were not. He had planned something that would scar me forever. He had me laying on his bed already and he had done his thing and jumped up quickly, put his clothes on, and immediately held me down to the bed while about five boys appeared out of nowhere. They were there to rape me. Two guys managed to rape me. I was kicking and screaming to let me go.

"Let me go! I don't wanna do this! Leave me alone, please. Please, stop."

My pleas fell on deaf ears.

I must have taken one deep breath in as the third guy thought he was about to get his turn. I kicked him in the nuts and screamed so loud a neighbor or somebody heard me and came knocking on the door and they all scattered. A few of them jumped out the windows, others hid. I don't know who this stranger was, but God knows I am thankful. I ran home and I never shared that with anyone.

I kept it inside. And that was when I began to keep the history of my abuses to myself.

CHAPTER 5

GLANCES OF REGRETS

"The shame, embarrassment, feeling of low self-worth, and scores of "labels" we give ourselves are not fitting. I am beginning to see how I had no control over the situation. He was a big man, I was a little boy."

— Charles L. Bailey Jr., In the Shadow of the Cross

Two days had passed since I was raped. The guys had been talking about me. One day, my brother caught glimpses of what they had done to me that made them never stop bragging and laughing and telling other people on the block what they had done to the "dumb little girl" next door. My brother set them straight, and they stopped, but that didn't change the violations and marks I lived with. I never spoke to that guy again.

It was uncomfortable to go outside many days, but I continued to hold my head up high. About five months had gone by since those events occurred. We had a new family that moved in on the block right across the street from us, which consisted of four sisters, two brothers, and their cousin. My mom became acquainted with them before I did. The oldest sister was in her 20s and would always be doing someone's hair out on their screened porch. My mom must have asked her if she did hair because later, she did microbraids for me and my sister.

This was how I met their brother. We both were in 8th grade getting ready to go into 9th grade that fall. He was like my first boyfriend. We would hang out every day watching TV in the living room, doing schoolwork, playing board games, and video games. Around that time, I enjoyed some B2K, and he knew it. Every time we would watch 106 and Park and a song came on, he would sing the lyrics because he knew the song. Nothing physical ever occurred between us. We were just hanging out with each other.

One day, while we were together, he respectfully and kindly said that he had to break up and stop talking to me because the guy across the street had told his sister and his sister told their cousin who told him that I had given somebody Head.

"What? What does head mean?" I asked.

He laughed derisively.

"C'mon, stop it. Everybody knows what that is," he said, shaking his head.

"Well, I do not!" I insisted.

He could see I was serious.

"A guy told me how he had sex with you," the boy confessed. He said so many things that my heart cannot even speak. But yet I kept my integrity. Never corrected anybody of the actual events because I had nobody, to confide in. I told no one that a group of nearly adult fellows ganged against a timid me. I simply allowed others to talk. By the time 9th grade ended, I had about four sex partners: one of which I dated a good six months.

Another lady and her two daughters moved into the vacant duplex unit upstairs. I would hang with the younger sister. Their mom was okay with them doing whatever they wanted. Many times, she and I would walk up to the white castle at literally one a.m. in a dangerous neighborhood. She would wear skimpy shorts and tight-fitted shirts. Sometimes she'd even let me wear some, too, because we couldn't afford much, and I always wore T-shirts and baggy jeans and ankle-length capris. The clothes I was seeing the girls in my area wear were new to me.

One day, while I went out with the girl, I remember talking to a guy and hanging with him. It was a late night, and I would walk like six blocks just to meet him.

Now do you understand why I shouldn't be alive now. I tell this to a lot of people who know me. It's God's mercy and grace that brought me here this far. I was so misguided. I was literally that girl who just did what others did. People who I've always considered to be friends were not. Everything I encountered I knew was not so good but at the time I didn't even know what half the stuff I was doing was called.

But I had no voice.

Who could I run to? Nobody. Who could I talk to? Nobody would ever believe me.

The only positive thing I remembered about 9th grade was being enrolled in a cosmetology course that was an elective that went towards high school and college credits. I began to learn how to do hair well. I knew how to do my hair in Micro braids, and French braids.

Also in 9th grade, I ended up dating a guy who was an all-star athlete who played varsity football. He was popular and well known, but that didn't really mean much to me. I still don't know what varsity means but I am guessing it had to be something great. He ended up breaking up with me by writing me a handwritten letter that did not entail his reasoning. After about a month went by, he approached me saying how he missed me, so we talked for about a month or two. I remember we were having sex in his bedroom one day and his father walked in on us. It was quite embarrassing. He walked me home.

Allow me to take a break from this story, please. I need it. It's been a good three weeks between now and the last paragraph because I felt so ugly and nasty.

"Hey," my son had walked into my bedroom where I have been writing. Have I told you he's already in high school? Well. He is. I'm not sure if I mentioned that. Shortly after I'd written down the number of sex partners I've had, that was when he came into the room. I have learned never to be ashamed of anything when I'm with my children. Whatever history I had had, it has brought me to what I am today— their mother.

"Son, it appears that your mother was a whole whore and a half mother."

This once again shows how God had his precious hands on me because I still had my life.

The story continues.........

One summer, my mother came in from work and said we were moving. I think that was the best moment I had during our entire time living there. We moved to Saint Paul. I had never heard of that city before moving out there. Now that my walk in this life is different and my eyes are open, God was moving us right along into a new season and out of the darkness.

All we had when we moved in was a folding table and two chairs. But, considering where we had just left, the floor looked just fine to me. My mother eventually got furniture a month later. Moving to a new city meant attending a new school. I would attend 10th-grade year with 9th-grade jitters in a sense. Our next-door neighbor had a daughter who happened to be enrolled in the same high school I was getting ready to attend, Arlington.

Here, I fit in right away. *What does that mean if you think about it?* I guess to me it meant I had come a long way from rarely or never being spoken to and never having long-term friends or close relatives that I had known all of my life. I was able to befriend others easily. Ranging from students that were well-known down to wholesomely good people that didn't have a name for themselves so to speak was a great thing.

What I am about to write next has nothing to do with high school, but I've discovered that the Lord had an amazing purpose and planned-out task for me. I only say that because, during one of my therapy sessions I made mention to her how when I grew into my youth, I did not know things.

"Sort of like the Virgin Mary," my therapist responded lightheartedly.

My mother kept our focus on things that children "should be." I went on to share with my therapist how I was never taught about hygiene. I learned a lot on my own. I remember being 11 and my sister being 9 and she and I would have to catch the city bus from Edina to Minneapolis to meet my mother. Back then there were no cellphones, we had a watch and written out instructions. I have come to realize how I just happened to fall victim unintentionally and came across people that were users, who were evil and took advantage of me.

In 9th grade, I became friends with Seeka, and I'm still in correspondence with her. One day I had met her downtown. Since then, she'd come to my house to spend the night. She was about a year or two older than me. While on the bus, she ended up being the one who told me what giving head meant and what it was. She goes on to say how she just slept with a guy, and he licked her you know what.

"He kissed me from head to toe girlllllll," she detailed, her face shining from the excitement of the memory. I still did not quite understand it, but how she explained it didn't sound like something I should have been told but it sounded exciting. I realized that it had been people who were around me that influenced the things I did. I have always been kind spirit, submissive, helpful, nurturing, and forgiving. Thinking about this right now, I'm only convinced of one thing: The world doesn't want us to be that way.

Seeka and I were speaking on the phone, and she said she had met a guy that was throwing a small get-together at his place and asked if I could accompany her because she didn't want to go alone. I never asked any detailed questions.

"Yes," I said. She was my friend.

Little did I know I was just a pawn. We had taken a cab from her house as her manfriend paid for it.

When we arrived at the place, it was filled with a mixture of men and females. I felt out of place. Music was playing, drugs were displayed, people were smoking, bottles of liquor were out. Not my vibe nor preference. I kept calm and held my peace and was respectful and engaged in conversation accordingly.

Did I listen to Hip hop and R&B? Yes. Did I enjoy activities like going to the movies and "normal" teenage hangouts that did not include adult things? Yes! I was all for the homecomings, the dances, etc.

I wasn't living under a rock. I wasn't just someone who publicized or even craved attention. I figured if you want to get to know me, approach me right. I just was not interested in those other types of things. I had never drunk or smoked. However, I remember when I was 13 and one of my relatives lit what they call a "blunt up" and told me to take a puff and I did. While at this gathering, I sat in a corner on this extremely huge sectional, alone while my friend was with her man.

One of the guys that were there came over to say hello. He was a gentleman. He asked my name. Did I want anything to drink? I said, sure.

I had a glass of hypnotic, which at the time I had no idea what it was nor what it was called as I made mention to the guy, I never drank alcohol. I was only 16. We were there until the late-night hours and then her man friend along with two of his friends walked her and me to the bus stop. Where I lived was not too far from where we were, and I told her I was not about to take a cab or bus back to her house across town. We roamed the streets of Downtown, Saint Paul. Not by my choice. They all were pretty drunk, and their behaviors were off balance.

I said nothing and watched things unfold. I felt like once again I was just an extra body for another so-called friend. She and I distanced ourselves from each other for a good 5-8 years after that. It would take us into mid-adulthood to reconnect— about a year before my daughter was born. She's been in my life a lot since then.

Although I was exposed to too many people, I never talked about them or judged anyone's life and if I did, it was unintentional as my life was as horrible as it could be. In the words of my amazingly great therapist:

"It's almost like you were going through trauma and not even being aware of the acts that you had done and participated in was supposed to be what society considers trauma."

CHAPTER 6

THE GIFT OF FRIENDSHIP

"A boy said, "Everybody is my friend." Beloved said, "No, not everybody can be your friend." – Santosh Kalwar.

I love to think that the places where we meet the people in our lives are important. The nightmares that marked my life and made it tumultuous came as a result of the people I met, and where I met them and let them into my life.

For my son's father, it began when I was in 8th grade. We met during a Youth Bible Study camp. We didn't kick off things from the start as it seemed we were pretty much young for things like that. But in the 10th grade, we reconnected and began dating. I could have sworn that things between us were meant to be all heaven and bliss. It turned out as I was wrong.

We dated from sophomore to right before senior year. We had some of the best of times, going on dates and doing all the things that lovers do to entice happiness. And then it ended abruptly. I was five months pregnant when the signs that he was cheating on me began to surface.

He was a very flirtatious guy, and he was shameless in his pursuits. That was how I came to know one of the girls he was cheating with. I had seen her around the neighborhood quite a lot. The girl knew I was pregnant.

"I'm carrying his baby," I said to her one day when I managed to meet her one-on-one. Ever since the rumors of his cheating began to swell, the girl had tried her best to make sure we didn't cross paths.

And now we did.

"I know. And I know he's your man. I've got no issues with that," the girl said, chewing gum.

I was surprised at her audacity. It seemed the girl studied the look on my face.

I had been prepared for this encounter for a long time. Just when I was about to strike her with violent words, she spoke.

"He is my cousin."

The words dropped into my body and melted whatever aggression building up inside of me.

That ended my confrontation. But my man knew I had met her, and it brought out the monster in him.

"You didn't have to do what you did," he said to me that evening. I was at his place.

"What are you talking about?" I asked, genuinely confused.

He drew closer to me, his eyes becoming red.

"You don't have to go questioning all the women in my life."

"I don't understand what you mean by that," I said.

"Stop lying!" I could see he was already getting worked up.

"Why do you have to go prying into my affairs.?"

"I wasn't prying!" I defended.

"Oh, so I'm the liar now?" he flared up, his hands slashing the air at nothing.

"Please, stop! This isn't wha..."

Before I could finish the words in my mouth, his right hand reached out and slashed the air again, very close to my face. I moved back at once, almost falling against the chair. It all happened in an instant.

My screams pierced the room and that would be the second time in my entire life that I had screamed like that.

"Shut your damn mouth!" he ordered. "You should have thought of that before doing anything stupid."

I kept my mouth shut once, expecting him to stop speaking in a strident tone. But it seemed he wasn't done with me. As soon as he saw me not making any moves, he raised his voice again, cursing vehemently. With each curse, his hand was slashing the air, as if he was imagining I was the one he was hitting. I had never seen him like that. Although he was not touching me physically, the pain in hearing his voice like that was describable. It was as if he was using his bare hands to uproot the hairs on my scalp.

"Please stop talking like that! You're making the baby upset!" I said, trying to stand up, while holding my pregnant belly.

"Mane I ain't trying to hear all that. Stay where you are before I lay my hands on you. I'm teaching you a lesson, for next time! So, shut the hell up!" he yelled again. I fell back on the bed, to avoid anything that could turn out to be worser than what his words already had echoed. The way my frustration had risen, it took only the grace of God that I didn't miscarry at that point. As he continued to pummel the air with his hands, his mouth didn't stop pouring all kinds of swearwords on me.

I stayed quiet, placing my hands over my belly, as if to protect my unborn child from his vocal violence. If I could not protect myself, nothing should stop me from protecting my baby.

I managed to raise my eyes to glance at his eyes, to see if there was any fragment of the man I loved in those hazel eyes. But all I saw towering above me, while I lay on the bed, my legs curled inwards out of terror, was a complete monster. His transformation was shocking and heartbreaking. There was no sympathy in his eyes. There was nothing in them that could whisper to me that, at least, he could still stay calm with his harsh words. How could he not think, for once, that I was carrying his child? How did I get here? Love brought me here. Or, stupidity!

At last, his hands stopped moving in the air. But the curses continued, a bit softly this time, as if he was trying to breathe, having exhausted his energy in the act. Then there was total silence in the room, except for my breaths, which were coming out with great difficulty.

And then he disappeared out of the room. It was as if something had taken over him, in the same manner that it had entered him before. I looked around the room after he was gone. The light in the room illuminated but all I saw was darkness– the darkness of my life. It stood before me in stubborn mockery.

I sat on the edge of the bed, crying, and silently screaming for help. In that state, my eyes closed and fell asleep.

When I woke up the next morning, I found the devil standing by the door smiling at me. When I saw him, tears began to form in my eyes again. I felt a deep sadness taking over. I was made to feel helpless.

He disappeared from the door and reappeared shortly after with a tray in his hands. He'd made breakfast for me.

"Good morning baby," he said, smiling affectionately, and looking deeply into my watery eyes. His hands ran gently across my face. I looked up at him. He was already teary. I opened my mouth to call his name, but he put a finger to his lips to keep quiet.

"Allow me to do the talking." He paused, his lips moving very hard as if looking for the right words to say. "I messed up big time last night. I… I… I don't know what came over me. I don't know. But whatever it was, I couldn't handle it then."

Silence.

"After I saw the way, you were last night, and that I was responsible for that, I felt so ashamed of myself that I had to leave the house immediately. I shouldn't have left you here alone. I'm so sorry."

While he was speaking, I was half-listening. My mind was roaming, taking by the winds of joy and sadness. I was happy because he had realized just how wrong he was and was apologizing for that. I was sad, afraid that he might turn out to repeat the same thing someday. But my joy and the love I had for him then, overwhelmed me.

Another moment of silence….

Finally, I reached out and held his hand, without saying a word. I caressed his palms while my other hand cleaned the tears from his eyes.

That morning, we made up. He'd go on to continue his flirtations with various women, even as our relationship became rocky until we finally reached rock bottom.

*   *   *   *

Intimate relationships or partnerships and marriages have remained inseparable from domestic violence. Ranging from slaps, hitting, shoving, emotional abuses, and other forms of assault, many relationships are twisted by intimate partner violence, even to the point of unavailability of sustainable interventions. More and more women frequently endure mild forms of violence until such small acts, turning into severe violence and aggression, damage them almost to the point of beyond repair. These are women with the real stories, yet they have no critical voice to speak for themselves.

Partner abuse is still contributing its share to some of America's major problems. The more women and men continue to face challenges in the forms of abuse with the people they chose to share their heart with, the more we should be expecting more homeless people on our street, physically injured people in our hospitals, the rise of death victims, billions of dollars lost in health care, loss of positive productivity at workplaces, and many more.

Perhaps, more than ever, this is the age where the necessary conversation on partner abuse and other forms of violence in relationships needs to be pushed into everyone's face.

Young men and women should be taught to be responsible in their relationships with others. They should expose themselves to ideals that advise against them from demeaning, assaulting, or excessively controlling the people they're in love with.

In my past, I have had to absent myself from my school due to abuses, change works, carry a lot of injuries, endure low self-esteem, live with a damaged personality, be afraid of daring new things or expose myself to situations where I could have been a better person a long time ago. I had made terrible choices and I suffered the consequences dearly.

*   *   *   *

Memory again.

Begin with friendship.

Here's Kay. Here's Mandy. Here's Kim.

Here's the thing with life that I have discovered gradually: Some people go through life without meeting that one person, or people, who would show them a part of themselves they had never seen before, a part of them that mattered and is crucial to how the rest of their lives might turn out to be like.

As for others, at each point they turn in life, they are fortunate enough to encounter the right people to "mirror" to them what they are, or what they could be.

The names above belong to my first friends in my new school, people whose earlier acceptance of me opened up my mind to discover new vistas of my life I was never aware existed. Even though we were as closed as all good friends could be, I hung out with Kay a lot and were more of a best friend to each other.

Kay was beautiful and even though I was struggling with low self-esteem, I found that we were similar in so many ways. She and I were mostly around the neighborhood together and did almost everything together.

Kay would never get her nails done without me doing the same. We were practically inseparable those days as I was always in the house. I never invited Kay over to my house. I didn't see the need to, and since I cherished what we had between us, I wanted to keep all my friends far from the drama at my place. My history before meeting them was not one I was ready to allow to blemish the joy I was deriving from being with them.

As my friendship with Kay blossomed, Mandy and Kim were also playing major roles in my life. I had one of my major head starts during the baby shower I had at Kim's house in honor of my son. They were wonderful to me, and it was one of the most memorable memories I had in life. They shared my happiness with me with genuine gestures and also provided the things my baby needed by the time he arrived.

Kim was everywhere and took charge of all the fun baby shower games we had and made sure everyone that came was entertained.

It seemed they were not done with it. Later, Mandy offered to become my son's God-mom. I was overwhelmed by the kind of love that my girls chose to shower on me, and I was grateful to God for bringing them into my life at a point where I needed them, and also for allowing God to use them to touch me and my baby.

While I had Kim, Kay, and Mandy as my friends, people didn't notice me until my senior year in high school.

The high school had an onsite daycare which I registered my son for. So, while I was in school, he would attend there. As for myself, my life had taken a dramatic turn since his birth. I began to appreciate and engage with life at every point I found myself facing. There was a parenting group that Amy, an amazing and kind lady led, that I got myself involved with. With them, I came to know of the joys, demands, and challenges that came with being a parent. The stories and experiences shared were shocking, beautiful, funny, heartbreaking, and at the same time, necessary and uplifting.

While all this was going on, my life was changing in two different places.

In school, I was still a shy person. But when I later ran for homecoming queen and failed to win it, I gradually came out of my shell.

Back at home, my mom and I still had not found a common ground to have a good relationship with each other. With what happened to me from childhood, and my experiences with my uncle at my Granny's, I slowly grew distant from her. I never disrespected her or called her names. My rebellion was never in such aspects. It was just that I had failed to see the necessity of being with her, or in her presence, or engaging with her as mother and daughter should. With my mother, I was just happy existing beside her, even when I didn't get to have the desired relationship with her.

As for my personal life, I continued to have sexual flings with different guys until I managed to graduate five months early from high school. Once that happened, I started to volunteer at the school daycare.

After that, I had no idea my life was about to change, forever.

*   *   *   *

What do abused women do with friendship? And what do they want?

I have come to an understanding that associating with strong women that one is proud to call friends can be a life-transformational thing to do, and also uplifting. It's one of our best support-base whenever we are going through things. Every human being desires a non-judgmental, less dramatic, and deeply understanding presence of another person around them.

Kim. Kay. Mandy.

They were unique. They had strong opinions. And even though they had formidable values, they were people who were ready to accept and accommodate others of different values. Maybe this was why we had it cool those days. They made me feel comfortable and gave me a different level of emotional support that I had never encountered before.

With every encounter of abuse that I faced with my man at home, associating with these girls made me stronger. They kept me in check and were brutally honest with me.

I believe that every woman passing through a phase such as this, truly deserves good friendship and a healthy support system. Since it could be a hard thing for some to do, women should make a duty to be intentional about making good friendships. Try out a coffee shop with someone who understands your pain. Even as you surrender yourself to God to help you, place yourself in strategic positions where good people are likely to meet you, and will have the right impact on your life.

This is important. It's important who you are connected to.

Here's the big deal. When things finally become too much for you to handle at home, most women leave and find support in the friendships that they had invested years in, rather than going back to their families.

That's what happened to me. When after the birth of my son I had nowhere to live, and I could no longer stay with his father, I packed our bags, took my son, and left.

Kay's arms were wide open, ready to accept me and my son.

CHAPTER 7

A ROUGH PATH DOWN THE ROAD

"People on the outside of situations like these often wonder why the woman goes back to the abuser. I read once that 85 percent of women return to abuse situations. That was before I realize I was in one, and when I heard the statistic, I thought it was because the women were stupid. I thought these things about my mother more than once." — Colleen Hoover, *It Ends with Us*

Let's say it as it is. Watching someone, especially someone that you love and cherish a lot, return to their abusive partner over and over again is exasperating!

There are hundreds of factors to explain why people in abusive relationships stay, or why they leave only to come back within a short time. But none beats this: "I thought I could change him." I would like to believe that women sometimes believe they are in love to the extent that even when it's bringing them nothing but pain after pain, they are too blind and unresponsive to see or feel that.

I understand that the things that happen to us in life could be peculiar to others. This is why it is important to state here early that my reasons for always coming back to my son's father might be different from those of other woman who has chosen to return to their man.

While I was with him, my thoughts weren't exactly mine. My mind was so distorted that I handed over the control of my thoughts to him. The import of this was that, soon enough, I began to live a confused and doubtful lifestyle, full of self-blame. I saw myself as the reason for him treating me the way he did. Whatever he did to me, I continued to see him as a well capable of changing someday, back to the person I fell in love with in the beginning.

Some days, alone in the house, as my son roamed around the room, I would look at him and wondered if I was making the right choice for both of us. I wondered if the path I was taking at that moment would lead us to our ruins. I would make up my mind to right all the wrongs. But as soon as I set eyes on my son's father, my mind would go back to its default setting. All I could think of was to do the right thing that would make him not cheat or be a hardcore yelling person towards me again. Whenever I left him, I would come back again with a strong belief that he had made peace with his demons and was now a changed man. I was always wrong!

Psychologically, I was wearing down with despair, guilt that seemed to melt itself into my skin. I was constantly ashamed and embarrassed at the things that I shouldn't have been ashamed of. I have always struggled with self-esteem as a child. It passed through schools, unnoticed, and gladly so. However, my self-esteemed became more damaged due to the degrading way my son's father kept treating me. I believed in him and lost faith in myself. Without him, I felt I would always be alone, worthless, undeserving of love, and a piece of baggage to people around me. I thought he was right.

His words, his manipulations, and the things he was capable of doing to me were so powerful that I lived daily in terror. I loved him. And I feared him. He was fully aware of his stronghold on me and manipulated it to his advantage.

One day, we were talking when he picked offense at something I said. Before I knew it, the words came out of his mouth:

"You're some ugly nightmare, you know, don't you?"

I have heard a lot of the worst things said about me. I have been raped, molested, abused, and all such degradations. I survived them all. But that evening, his words made a huge impact on me. Because of this and other things, I was living in fear of him. I also began to realize that even my son was not safe with him, since he was witnessing at that young age the way I was being yelled at by his father. It was a situation I would never want my son to witness until he was fully conscious of their effects on his life.

While I had been contemplating leaving him for the final time, I was held down by my desire to help him change. I was seeing him as a child losing his way and I, the parent, rising to lead him right back on track. Memory. My memories of all the good times we've had stuck with me. And the more they did, the more resolute and convinced I became that my love was sufficient enough to make him change. All I had to do was to let him see that I still loved him, despite everything happening. I was fully and unquestionably committed to him. If he was too weak to fight for us, my strength would see us through. I would fix him. I would teach him to love me again. And to heal him, and sustain our relationship, I tried to find reasons why he was acting that way towards me. I failed again.

*　　*　　*　　*

PAUSE.

I will keep repeating this, you know. When it started, I blamed myself for his ways. He was always charming with everyone. I wondered why it was different with me, I became supercritical of myself and my decisions. I would always wish that whenever someone visited us, they would stay a little longer because he was happy. I tried to learn from them, so I could make him happy even if it was for a little while. I couldn't understand why I'd be scolded for some random mistake at every chance he got. I couldn't fathom what the heck I was doing wrong that was unusual from when we were all loved up.

Oh dear, that's manipulation right there, I know. One common trait of abusers is to control. Everything. I said that. You know that already. From your thoughts— how you express them to how you basically live your life. They make it look like they are the good guys while you are the slimy villain compelling them to turn bad. I had felt all these ways. Being here today writing this, it still seems unbelievable that I was the survivor, the overcomer that emerged with a miracle. I took nothing for granted.

IF I LEAVE, WHERE WOULD I GO?

This was one of the many questions that kept passing through my mind. I had invested so many years loving him. It was all I knew how to do. I couldn't go back to my family. My past experiences I had erased any thoughts I had ever entertained to go back home and begin again. I was surrounded as a girl by animals who had their animalistic ways on me in many ways that weren't appropriate for a girl still in the age of innocence.

Here I was, limited by enough money to care for myself and my child, broken by my past, and afraid to let my son grow up without a father. I wanted him to know what it feels like to have a man that would call him "son," or "my child." I wanted him to play in the garden with his father, to walk the streets of Minneapolis with his father holding his hands. I wanted him to have pride that he was never like so many children running the streets who have never set eyes on their fathers. I count myself as one of those children.

I wanted my son to have what I never had. I wanted my history to be different from his history. I wanted his life to be filled with love, kindness, and the joys of family.

For these reasons, and many more, I stayed.

*   *   *   *

For the next few years, I dated my son's father on and off. My friends were exhausted by it all. Kay and I had continued to be friends for those years. And when I finally got the courage to say I was over him, I took my son and left.

I went on to have another relationship again. And, again, I had to leave.

Still there was nowhere I could call my home. My mother had been moving us from one city to another, shifting our bodies from one shelter to the other, in the name of survival. That wasn't the kind of life I wanted for my son. Like always, Kay stepped in and played a role at that critical stage of my life. She invited me to stay with her. I was already done with high school.

*　　*　　*　　*

The Abuser's Working Tools and His Game

One out of four women has suffered from severe physical abuse. The number likely doubles over if you add verbal and emotional abuse. Women who have been abused suffer and live-in intimidation, humiliation, isolation, and fear that not only diminishes their sense of self-worth and esteem but also threatens their sanity. Degradation is one common character of the abuser, perpetually tearing you down sometimes in front of the kids, relatives, or even strangers. The trait of the abuser is fear and intimidation, gifted at threatening to harm or punish you. Control. Intimidation. Subjugation. Punishment. Isolation. These are the working tools of the abuser.

My abuser was smooth and sleek. I used to think it was anger. I mean, when you're angry you say mean and hurtful things to people which you probably later regret but, No. My abuser wasn't ever like that. He was in complete control of his senses. He had implicit mind games designed to question my sanity and judgment.

Have you checked out your abuser?

He will never play fair. His game is to gain total control over you. He is out to make you feel hopeless and alone, destroy your self-esteem and worth which eventually leads to anxiety and depression.

He is out to seep you in fear, guilt, shame, and intimidation until he wears you down and keeps you right under his thumb.

You could be smart and intelligent and believe that no one will take advantage of you... I mean, you're never going to let anyone do that to you. There are a lot of women who have thought the same way as you. Until they meet a man who sweeps them off their feet. At first, your independence is not threatened and you're given a false sense of it. Soon, you begin to have arguments over things you have no idea where they came from. When it happened to me, I really began to think I was the problem. that I allowed my stubbornness to get the better of my relationship.

Back to you. You're still on the radar.

When you would fight, he would point out all the previous mistakes that led you to this point. You'd ask yourself where's the gentleman you knew disappeared to. He'd come apologizing with roses and kisses after each fight. For the next few days, you'd be really happy but you're in constant fear of what would happen to you when the next episode of madness burst. And it did always burst sooner or later.

If he stays late-night (and he usually does), he begins to steal money from you. When you confront him, he'll promised you it was all for y'all's future. If you ask for receipts he'd flare up and accuse you of not trusting him enough while he was doing everything for you, investing "our money" so you'd be better off financially tomorrow and pursue your dreams. All that was lies from the pit of hell.

I went through all of this with my man right until I left.

*   *   *   *

The first time I was with Kay, everything was perfect between us. But after some time, I began to notice some unusual changes in Kay.

The year was 2010 and it came to usher in the tumult that would finally rock the friendship between Kay and me. My son had been attending her stepmom's daycare when I first started staying with her.

If you recalled, I said Kay and I were inseparable as we went everywhere together. For anyone who knew us, we were known to be the best of friends. It was disturbing that Kay started going to certain events without inviting me. I loved the practical idea of giving people their personal space. I gave Kay that. But this was different. The places she was visiting were places that we would ordinarily have gone together if things were truly going on well between us. They weren't.

"How come you don't invite me to places anymore?" I asked her one day when she was about to head out.

"Come on, girl, I'm so sorry. I just thought they were places you wouldn't feel like going to anymore."

I'd let that passed, hoping that things like that wouldn't happen again, hoping she would remember I still missed the days when we did almost everything together.

But the same thing kept repeating itself, and whenever I brought that up, Kay went ballistics on me. In the end, we gradually grew apart.

This is my confession: I give myself completely. When I'm in a relationship with anyone, I'm fully into that person. There's no doubt or question about that. It is this completeness and surrender that I also brought into all my relationships all those years. I placed my focus on that person meaning that anything or anyone else becomes secondary. I suffered from this a lot.

I know that there are quite a lot of people out there who love the same way. There's nothing wrong with that. What is wrong is when you're investing all of yourself in the wrong man. Today, I can confidently say that all the men I met those years were wrong for me. I had no second thought about this.

Whenever my relationships ended, I would begin to find a place to heal again. With no one to run to, I would seek out my friends again, and fall into their hands for support.

*　　*　　*　　*

Being with the Wrong Men for the Wrong Reasons

There are a lot of reasons some women chose to be with the wrong men, and all for the wrong reasons. I have ticked all the boxes throughout my life experiences.

Each one of us fears loneliness. Nobody truly wants to be alone. It is this fear that eats into the minds of women like me who have had to endure a lot in the hands of a man. Any love that is capable of hurting you should never be yours. We know. But fear would never allow us to let go. So, we stick with the wrong man, for the wrong reason, until it becomes too late one day.

It would take me a long time to know never to be afraid of being alone, never to be ashamed of my own company. By accepting this fundamental truth, I was able, through God's amazing grace, to build an independent and formidable life for me and my children.

To be lonely is not the problem. What we do with our loneliness is what matters. There are some who use their loneliness to develop their self-esteem and to sit in a single place to deliberate on their most important life choices.

I accepted myself. And I made it a duty to myself to stop trying to change people. The idea that we can change people has done us more harm than good. I gradually grew up to refuse to be in a relationship with a man that I have to "fix" at each point of our lives together. It is not my duty. It is his's, and if that change fails to come from him, there's nothing that I or any other woman could do to help.

If you're a woman that has had terrible experiences at the hands of men, you need to accept the fact that no man has the right to approach you to "fix" him. There are always heartbreaks, conflicts, and injuries that would mar you for the rest of your life.

*   *   *   *

My daughter's father and I met in 2008. Our relationship lasted for the next eight years. Like all previous relationships, I was also standing at the edge of the cliff in this one. Each of them was peculiar. But with him, I came to learn the intricacies involved in drug dealing, as he was himself a big-time drug dealer. I didn't know about this before I started dating him. It was quite much later that I found out who he actually was and what he did for a living. But by that time, I was too far gone into him. By now, you must have realized how hard it was for me to walk out of that relationship. Even when I knew him deeply, it was too late for me to back out. Our relationship was supposed like the ones I had before meeting him– a fling. But, before we both knew what was happening, it took longer than I expected.

His name was Benis. He was a good-looking man that it would be hard to pin him down as a drug dealer. Benis and I kickstarted things between us on a very good note, that I was hopeful that, finally, here was a man that would treat me well.

Three months after dating, he told me he wanted me to meet his mom. That was huge! I met Benis' mom a few days later.

She was a woman full of zest and ran a daycare just outside of her house. She was nice to me as she was to everyone around her. But behind all that niceness, she had a strict vibe dwelling in her. One day, I asked Benis why she was like that.

"She used to be a businesswoman," he replied. "That was some years back. You know how those business people are," he added, and we laughed.

Benis' mom and I grew closer. Later, I began to help out as a worker in her daycare until I got a job. My new job was at the Mystic Lake Casino. I worked there even as I made one last decision to attend college to become a medical assistant. I made a stubborn commitment to that decision and stood by it. Benis' mother would watch over my son until I got off work at midnight.

It was around this time that the mental and physical abuses started in my relationship with Benis. Like most men that I had dated before him, I never knew what came over him and how unaware of the changes taking over him. I knew he was a drug dealer. But he was never violent with me when we started dating, until now.

One night, I came back quite late and entered the house. I knew my baby would be sleeping by then. I went up upstairs where I would find him doing just that. I stood there, watching him. And then I felt as if someone was standing behind me. I turned sharply. It was Benis.

"Dang it," I swore. "You scared me?"

"You came home late again," he said. I could feel the tenseness in his voice. It was also accusatory.

"It's work, Benis," I said. I was already too exhausted to engage him.

"And what else?" he asked, still looking at me. By now, he'd stood by the door, blocking the exit.

"What do you mean by what else?"

"You seeing someone out there?"

"How could you even think of something like that, baby?"

I had not taken another breath after those words when his hand landed on my cheeks. It was a stroke of sheer luck that he missed my eyes.

Without saying a word, he left the room immediately. I turned to see that my son had not awakened.

And that was how it began.

For the time that I was with him, I was on my toes. He became so mentally, emotionally, and physically abusive that I had begun to return to the shadow of a past I was trying to escape from. Some days, I woke up afraid of what terror the day would bring my way. To escape everything, I immersed myself into work and school where I managed to have some peace.

Finally, when I had given birth to our daughter, things calmed down between us. We were back to our normal selves as if nothing had ever come between us capable of causing the other person great damage.

It was only after I gave birth to my daughter that I realized I had never truly loved Benis. I had been with him all these years, and it was surprising that it took me this long to realize that.

I had no regrets about that.

Chapter 8

Breakup: Reconciliation

"The road to heaven isn't much of a road," he was saying. "It's more like a dusty trail, roughly cut out through the underbrush. Most people don't even notice it. It doesn't look like a path at all, so they walk right by. — Bonnie Grove, *Talking to the Dead*

I had been indoors for days. It was a deliberate choice as I needed to have some time to myself. On the fifth day, I came out of the house and decided to go to a beauty supply shop. As it would appear to be, something must have been guiding me.

I exchanged a few words of greetings with some of the people in the shop. I had not sat down for a minute when someone called my name. I turned around.

It was April.

I screamed and stood up from where I was sitting to hug her. We embraced each other as if our lives depended on it. When I left my home that afternoon, I had no idea I would be seeing her. April and I hadn't seen each other since I stopped working at the call center job where I had met her early in 2015.

I've had a lot of breakups in my life, especially romantic ones. I had a rare ability to let people walk out of my life. But, some nights, realizing that friendship breakups were usually the hardest,

I stayed awake thinking about all the people that I truly cared about who had walked out of my life at one point or the other.

I thought about Mandy, Kim, and Kay a lot. My breakup with them, even though I hadn't admitted it to anyone, was quite devastating. I was constantly flooded by memories of the time we spent together. I knew that people weren't meant to be in our lives forever. But it was incredibly intimidating to think that I had moved on really well without them.

Right now, I looked deep into April's eyes, and it was clear to me that she had missed me as much as I did. She continued to acknowledge my presence in the room, momentarily unable to say anything.

"Wassup beautiful?" I asked, with genuine concern, love, and a hunger to know what she had been up to. "I never knew I would see you again," I added excitedly. It was as if years had gone by between us, when it was simply a matter of months.

"God knows I missed you," April replied, and we both laughed.

We had spent some incredibly beautiful moments together since we became friends and it was impossible not to know the right thing to say to make the other person laugh. We had spent hours, and even more, until the day turned darker, just to be in each other's presence.

Like always, April was full of life, and I could see that nothing much had changed about her. She was still the same April, still one of my favorite people on the planet. The moment we reconnected, it was like all the shades of distance and silence that had existed between us suddenly gave way. It was as if we were back just where we had begun, all over again, and nothing in the world could come between us. We looked at each other so deeply. April knew me, as much as I knew her. She was one of the few people on earth that we could say a thousand words to each other by simply looking at each other's eyes while letting our feelings speak for us. It was as if no one in the entire world meant as much as April meant to me. Sometimes, whenever I looked at the things that had happened to me, I wondered if my life would have had any speck of interesting, exciting, and emotional moments without April taking the ride along with me when she did when we first met. Even though we had our fair share of differences on some occasions, and had even spent some time without communicating with each other, April was part of the window through which I had seen the outside world and discovered a lot about my human nature.

After some time of few talks, she held my hand as we got out of the beauty salon until we were right outside. That day, we spent a great deal of time with each other, catching up on all the things that had happened to each of us while the other was away.

No matter how hard we try, our lives would always turn out differently from that of our closest friends. We make different life plans. One of us is likely to move out of state and meet completely different people down the road. It would take the grace of God, who is always kind to see that only the right people surround His children, to keep in touch with each other and maintain intimacy.

I used to believe that longtime friends who had not seen each other for months, and even years, could reconnect for a reason, even if that reason is unknown, at first, to both. But God is working His magic work. This was what I came to believe after April and I reconnected.

In October of 2015, on the night of my birthday, I made a decision that would determine how the next step I would be taking in life. Breaking off from my daughter's father was something I should have done a long time ago. I delayed because at the time while I was still with him, I had no one to look after my children. I was practically alone in the universe, with no friends to turn to for help.

The day I broke up with Benis, I made sure that my children were in a safe place before he tried to harm them. He didn't take it well. He tried to reason with me, begging me with tears in his eyes. When he realized that I'd made up with my mind, he turned to threats and demeaning words to make me feel that I was nothing without him.

"Tell me, how would you survive out there?" he asked.

"I will find a way to do so," I said. "I always do."

"Let me tell you something since it seems you're not thinking straight," he drew closer. I took a few steps back. "You're only being selfish here. You're not thinking about the damn kids at all!" he barked.

"It's because of them I'm doing what I'm about to do," I replied immediately.

Benis hated confrontation, even when it seemed he was in the wrong. All it would take for him was the smallest confrontation. As soon as I replied to him, I didn't realize when his hand was wrapped around my neck as he held it tight, almost choking me out of breath. Tears began to spiral from my eyes.

"I… can't… breathe…" I managed to push the words out of my mouth. My hands were holding tight to his arms, trying to free myself.

"I leave bitches! Bitches like you don't get to leave me. And one more thing, don't you ever dare speak to me that way again! You think you've got a well-grown ass to survive out there in those streets without me now, huh? Fine, let's see how you'll make it out there without me! Let's see!"

Then as suddenly as he held my neck, he released me. I took some minutes to exhale deeply moving backward from him.

He glared at me before he quickly put his shirt on and left the house as if nothing had just happened between us.

I swore that it was the last time that he and I would ever be together again.

* * * *

Benis and I had broken up for six months now. Around the corner where I lived, I discovered there was a call center where I could get a job. It was a job that gave me time to be able to look after my children unlike before.

I was still enjoying my friendship with April. As I mentioned before, I believe the Lord brings certain people back to our lives for a reason. At the same time that our friendship began to flourish again, I became involved with a guy who took me as his prey. He had a hold on me that no man before him ever had on me.

"That guy is not good for you, girl," April told me one day. We were at her place when we started discussing my relationship. April had been complaining about my relationship for a long time. Of all the friendships I had made along the years, it was April that had the highest sense of foreboding. She had a flair for knowing when something bad was about to go down. And now, she was not okay with my new boyfriend.

At this point in my story, I'd like to say more about April. This is because she came back in my life at this very strategic point. It was God that sent her to me, and I refuse to believe otherwise.

The fact that April was outspoken and blunt with the truth had made many people uncomfortable around her, but that was the same thing that I admired her for. Her words were usually imprinted on me and had the right impact on me.

84

It was easier to get offended by her bluntness and straightforward approach to reality. Yet, April had remained one of the gentlest and most available people I've ever had. She always knew what to say. She always knew what to do. She always knew the right questions to ask, even if those questions were certain to be a bit scratchy.

Every few weeks, we would always make out time to be with each other, despite our busy schedules. When she finally opened up to me that she was not okay with my relationship, I knew I had to start paying attention. And to take caution at once!

I had made many decisions that I regretted in my life. and I had paid the cost for them. Right now, whatever I would be doing with my life, I wouldn't want anything or anyone to harm my children or me. I wanted their innocence to protect them. I wanted to protect their innocence.

However, I was already too far gone, attached to my new boyfriend that I couldn't take immediate action. The young man had a stronghold over me. His controlling behavior was so strong over me that I appeared to have no strength to defy him. While we were dating, I discovered that he secretly had knowledge of everywhere I went– the time I got there, whom I was with, and when I left. He was stalking all of my moves. It was terrifying. Still, I continued to be with him. We'd hang out in many places around us while I kept my children somewhere safe.

"How about I come to your house one of these days?" he asked me.

In the two weeks that we had been meeting, I was yet to invite him over to my place.

I didn't think about it, as I made no big deal out of it.

"Sure, why not?"

That evening, he appeared at my doorstep with his clothes. Still, I made nothing out of it, as I saw it as a harmless gesture. I was so madly into this guy that all my thoughts seemed to be distorted. I confessed that in my search for love, I had destroyed some things. I had overlooked the warning signs because I felt I was no longer attached to an 8-year abusive relationship. I was enjoying my freedom so much that I had no idea I was unwittingly walking into another trap of disappointment, wasted time, harmful emotions, and self-destruction. It would take me some time to realize all of this until it was almost too late.

I had been lying to myself for years, refusing to go into the strength within me to no longer give any man control over me. Every time I did this, I suffered from it. Since I started seeing him, it was one lie after another. And with each lie, my life seemed to come crashing down around me. I had passed through enough crises to the extent that I was almost non-functional. No one had the power to save me except me. I had the sole responsibility of cleaning up my mess. The sooner I did that, the better it would be for me and my children.

While I was with this guy, I was totally at his mercy, doing everything he asked me to do. I was giving him my money and he was a big spender. Each time he asked for some cash from me, if I gave him an excuse that I didn't have it, he would go into a fit of rage. I would bend to his will, giving him what he wanted.

I noticed that he was trying his best not to leave my house. And his clothes were increasing in number. He was practically living with me! His presence was telling on me both financially and psychologically.

Throughout my life, I had learned to live with my discomfort. I would let things that would normally push other people to madness get through to me without driving me insane. While all of this was going on, I was internally seeking an escape from the pain I was going through inside.

As this guy continued to reveal his true colors with time, I found out that I was "tolerating" his excesses. He still had control over me. The hardest thing, I had come to believe, is learning to be honest in telling ourselves that it is time we let go of people we love who are causing us nothing but pains and constant degradation.

When I let him go, it was not because of his humiliation and treatment of me. It was my children.

"Are you deaf to the streets or what?" April asked me one afternoon. Her question was so sudden that I turned and looked at her. Defiant, she tilted her head to the side and looked back at me.

"What do you mean, April?" I asked back. I honestly had no idea what she was trying to say. Judging by the tone of her voice, it was clear she had bottled this inside her for some time. And that was something about April. She knew we were close. However, she also respected the boundaries between us and the need for privacy. Sometimes, she did not tell me some things she felt, as an adult, I was capable of figuring things out on my own.

It was obvious I couldn't figure out whatever she was about to tell me.

"Fine. Word on the street is that your new man abuses children. And I see no reason why you should keep him around your kids."

My eyebrows were on fleek and arched, and my eyes widened as I stared at April, unable to say a word.

I always knew he was never a saint and that I was capable of surviving his excesses. But what about my children? Wasn't it also my responsibility to make sure they were safe and protected? I was downcast and disappointed with myself. In my foolishness, I had brought my children to danger in more ways than ever.

"I guess you didn't know that after all," April said, rubbing my shoulder. "The better you leave that bastard, the better it would be for you and the kids."

I still wasn't saying a word. April understood how I was feeling. "Hey, hey, look here," she insisted. I looked up at her. "I seriously wouldn't want you to go down that path of blaming yourself. We all make mistakes, girl. Now, do something about it."

To this day, I still don't know how things would have turned out if April hadn't revealed the truth about him to me. My God! I made so many mistakes those days, and each day I realized just how much God was saving me! What would have become of my children? It was hard imagining the damage he would have done to their lives by the time it was too late for me to realize his true identity.

That evening, after I left April, I decided there and then to cut off all ties with him. During this period, it occurred to me that the more I tried to stay away from him, the more I made everything worse. Even though I ended up breaking free from his mind control, it seemed we were not yet done with each other or, more appropriately, he wasn't done with me.

At first, he kept begging and sending me several messages to take him back. I didn't. I had made up my mind and nothing, I convinced myself, was going to make me come back to him. I might have been joking with my life in my search for love and companionship. But I was not stupid enough to joke with, or endanger, my children's lives. They're too precious for me to do that to them.

At the point where I had decided to go separate ways from him, I had no idea what he was about to do, and that he was not willing to let me go that easily. At least, not without some drama. Seeing that the barrier between us had become visible and unshaken, he became a core stalker and followed me everywhere I went, even to the places that I was not expecting to see him.

"You need to stop following me around," I turned abruptly one day and shouted at him, careful not to draw people's attention to us. It was clear to him that I found his presence quite offensive. I had also begun hating myself for being so blind to not see him for who he truly was.

"I just want to talk to you," he said, drawing closer to me.

"I don't want to talk to you," I emphasized. "Please, stay away from me!"

When I left him that day, I didn't see him for two days. Each time I was outside, I would turn over my shoulders to make sure no one was following me. I was aware of what dangerous stalkers like him could do and April and I had discussed that several times. For one, I was afraid he would start threatening and harassing my children, or attack either of them (or even me) somewhere and cause them sexual or physical injury.

But he was yet to do any of that. Still, I found his nonviolent stalking a depressing thing to deal with. The fear that anything could happen to me at any point in time was stealing my life and my joy. I was reducing my social life and losing confidence in myself even as it became overwhelming to isolate myself.

Unable to take this anymore, I confided in April, who was following every development. A month later, I went to the police and reported him, explaining in detail everything that had happened between us and my relationship with him. They placed a restraining order against him.

All of this still didn't deter him from stalking me. He continued to do that for a year until I finally stopped seeing him around.

The experience with my ex had so much broken me that it felt as if a large part of my life had been taken away from me, never to be recovered again. I hated myself more. Why was it that each time I thought I was getting control of things, I would eventually make mistakes, usually avoidable ones, that would bring me right back to where I had been?

It would take me a strong sense of faith and self-forgiveness before I was able to free myself from my guilt. One night, I came back home, locked the door, went into my room, and cried for about an hour.

It was probably the last time I cried that hard. And it felt good. After that, I decided there and then that I was done with men. At least, for now. I needed a long time to get my mind right.

If only I knew what was ahead coming for me.

Chapter 9

Still A Small Distance Towards Happiness

"I advise you to stop sharing your dreams with people who try to hold you back, even if they're your parents. ... if you want to be EXTRA-ordinary- you will not get there by hanging around a bunch of people who tell you you're not extraordinary. Instead, you will probably become as ordinary as they expect you to be."

— Kelly Cutrone, *If You Have to Cry, Go Outside: And Other Things Your Mother Never Told You*

Towards the sunset of 2015, I had become increasingly afraid of the outside world. Because of this, I had spent almost a week staying indoors. This choice was also partly a deliberate one as I was trying so hard to focus solely on myself and face the hardest decisions of my life that wanted to be made. Here's a small truth: We are always making decisions. We cannot completely make up a single decision that could cover up for all other decisions that we had to make in the future. With each step we make, as we progress in life, we reach a particular point where we had to take a breath and make another decision.

This was the point I found myself.

After days of being indoors, I decided to face the outside world once again. There was a danger out there focusing on destroying me and posing a bigger threat than I could ever imagine. It seemed that whatever I did, I did it wrong and it was only bringing me closer and closer to that danger. Yet, I had to go out. Whatever happened, let it happen. Amid my biggest fears, I had the presence of courage that convinced me that everything would finally be okay.

The first place that I visited was the spa pedicure salon. I didn't even think about it. I simply decided that that was where I was heading as if some mysterious force was guiding me. All my life, I had come across things that had the potentials to either harm me or protect me, to point in the wrong direction or guide me in the right place to go, to bring me sorrow, or reward me with happiness.

At the spa pedicure salon, I saw Molly, whom I came to know through a program my high school social worker referred me to for teen girls with children. She took me places and activities. I also hung with her beautiful family. They didn't mind a whiney baby that traveled with me. She was like a second mom or it at least to me felt that she was motherly. She taught me how to cook. She encouraged me. Out of the kindness of her heart, she stayed in touch with me after high school. She also attended my high school graduation – although we drifted away as far as communicating for a few years, we came back stronger reconciling that day. My mentor/friend she showed me that life didn't have to stay how I was currently experiencing it. She never judged me in any way. I stayed with her, and after a few talks, I said goodbye to her and left. I walked around a little without any direction on my mind. About an hour later, I returned to the house and watched December passed by quietly, ushering my life into another new year of wondering about the uncertainties coming towards my life.

*　　*　　*　　*

It seems that everyone used me for their personal gain and benefits. My adulthood life had begun at the age of 19 with the dramatic relationship I had with my daughter's dad. I would dedicate the next eight years of life to him, sheltering all his wants and all. I had not lived much for myself. From the roommate drama and false rumors spoken by Seeka to all failed relationships in my life, the year turned, I looked at my life and decided there and then that this year was my year of being selfish with myself. I was letting go of all the things I felt were holding me back. Lacking inhibitions, I stopped myself from being so self-conscious and unable to let myself relax and act in a way that would bring me joy. I was comfortable with my environment and became even more confident with the people around me.

January 2016.

I began frequenting bars again to hang out with my friends. There was no fear holding me back and I had gradually identified all the points where I could easily be broken by people. My feelings, my thoughts, and my fantasies were becoming wild and almost domineering. I was going at everything with sheer abandon as if I was trying to make up for a lost time. And, dear God, I was.

I was driving towards creating an incredible collection of memories.

My friends noticed this. And they loved it. I understood why. I had passed through a long period living in the shadows of other people, being constantly afraid and always vacating places centered around growth, purpose, and fulfillment. Little did I know that the path I was taking was yet too far to take me towards these three things.

March 2016.

I had known Derrick since we were little. He was Kay's older brother. Derrick had always been casual with me, as we used to have little talks whenever I visited Kay. But there was nothing serious in our encounters. When my life took the momentum of its own and we all began to embrace adulthood, Derrick and I briefly lost touch.

I began to upload videos of myself twerking on Snapchat in March. I had forgotten what inspired me to start doing that. But one day, I was alone in the house when this song "Booty Me down," came on and I found myself dancing vigorously. Soon enough, I began to twerk. If it was a few years ago, I wouldn't have done what I did: Post it on Snapchat. But this was 2016. And I was no longer the same woman I used to be all those years ago. I was more adventurous than I had ever been. I took the video recording and uploaded it on Snapchat stories. The video had a lot of engagements. After that, I began to post more videos, enjoying the attention and everything.

A few weeks after I began posting, I went to Snapchat one day and saw a message sent to me about an hour ago. I opened it. It was from Derrick, Kay's brother.

> *"Wow! This is crazy! I never knew you could do this!*
> *This is massive & so beautiful!"*

When I read the message, I could visibly see Derrick's excitement. It felt different coming from him. I responded to his message and a few minutes later, he replied to me. That was how it began.

For the next two months, we continued to exchange messages on Snapchat. One evening, I logged into Snapchat quite late and saw Derrick online. A few seconds later, his message popped up. He wanted my number. We exchanged numbers and immediately his call came in. That night, we spoke for a long time and talked about various things. Even for the first day, especially after a long time of not seeing each other, conversation with Derrick wasn't that hard at all. If anything, it was as if we had spent the entirety of our childhood talking to each other. And this wasn't true.

June 2016

After I had gone into teaching, I attained a certificate in 2016 I was working as an infant/preschool teacher until 2018. One morning, I witnessed something that turned my bones to ice. The daughter of the school owner was abusing one of the infants under her care. I was furious and I knew I had to report it. Even though this would stand in the way of my job where I was also making good money, I was willing to sacrifice it as long as I was sure it would save a child's life. I reported it and then lost the job.

I went from one dead-end job to another from 2018-2019. It wasn't what I was planning for. I wanted something that could help me advance in my career.

July 2016

We became a couple. Being with Derrick convinced me that this was my first "real relationship" as I never felt like I had been in one before. I was happy. I was content and pleased with my life, and everything seemed to be falling into place. I was introduced to the diverse ways of experiencing life. Derrick loved the outside world, and we went to as many places as possible, including a trip to Vegas. On weekends, we would go the cinema to watch movies. On other days, you could find us bowling, or at the golf court. We made sure we visited some of the major bars in the city.

Relationship!

I see true relationships as a place of value where two people in love, who respect, love, and are committed to each other, could find comfort, sustenance, and trust that could be lacking in their immediate world.

There are a lot of people who have chosen to keep their relationships private. Apart from the need to keep their motivations pure, people might also want to keep their relationship private to protect it, far away from the impact and sentiments of the outside world who might not understand the need for them to be together.

Even as memories are being made, emotions are becoming solid, and experiences are gathering, we are constantly keeping the most precious moments of our lives safe from shame, exploitation, and dishonor.

I wanted everything that pertains to my private life this time around should reign true, and nothing in the entire world is allowed to impair it— not even my immoderations.

I was wrong.

*   *   *   *

In April 2017, I decided to make my relationship with Derrick public. I was not hoping to present us to the world as the ideal couple to be admired and adored. If anything, I always tried to shelter my life from drama and constant public interrogation. I was usually quite unsuccessful in this.

My reason for relieving my relationship with Derrick was simple: I could not keep it private forever, even if I wanted to; so why not?

All along, while I was dating her brother, Kay didn't know. It was intentional. I wanted to make sure of the things that Derrick, and I shared; I wanted to be certain it would work out between us before I let the world know.

I have been disappointed by the people who I thought cared for me. Where I expected to be understood, I was given judgment. Where I expected to be loved, I was hated. Where I expected acceptance, I was rejected. This was the trajectory of my life as far as I remembered it. This was what happened between me and Kay.

It was the second week of April when I told Kay that Derrick and I were dating. We had just come out of a clothing store and found a nearby café that was quiet for us to talk. Before now, I informed her that I would love to tell her something. I could have done so by calling or texting her. But I wanted to do so in person. No one knew my history as much as she did.

Kay was quiet for some time, surrendering the atmosphere to such tenseness that had never existed between us.

At last, she muttered: "How could you?"

"I… I don't understand, Kay. How could I what?"

"How could you agree to date him?"

"He's different! And I'm happy with him in a way that I have never felt in a long time," I defended. I wondered if I was right to have told Kay all these things.

"You have betrayed me," she said quietly and stood up, leaving me. I didn't leave immediately. I sat down for a while trying to process what just happened. I couldn't make meaning of anything. Was Kay, by her question, suggesting that I was too damaged to date her brother? Was I unworthy of his love? I had passed through so many phases of my life to witness people seeing and telling me I wasn't worthy. I could live with that. But there was no way that I could muster the strength to endure Kay's action.

Our friendship should have been enough container to hold in whatever each of us was passing through. It should never be seen providing space for judgment. Instead, I was wishing for a connection where I could be accepted with my flaws and all. I am a very mindful person and little things, especially disappointments by friends get to me easily. For a long period, it was hard for me to remain the same again after what happened between Kay and me. I saw her as a very miserable person posing as my friend but who would be happy to see me in pain rather than rejoice at the goodness in my life. One day, I prayed to God for my life and for all the people that He had used to touch me positively. After that, I kept my distance away from her for years. By keeping her out of sight and out of mind, not knowing whatever was happening in her life, I had begun to take the first tangible steps to heal my heart from her betrayal.

One of the lessons I learned from childhood and had continued to use to this day was that I should keep my personal life out of the public eyes. If anything, this should be one of the many lessons that kids from African American families learn to do. Our concerns are our concerns. We never know who in the world is truly happy for us and the fortune that's coming our way.

Although I knew I couldn't do so forever, I sometimes wished I had kept my relationship with Derrick private as long as possible; perhaps, until he, too, was strong enough to weather the storms with me. This was because, after the incident with his sister, things between Derrick and I turned outside down at once. The excitement that was there in our relationship gradually began to wane.

My communication with Derrick went down and I began to see little of him. Like all men getting disinterested in a relationship, he started coming up with different and silly excuses about why we couldn't meet as planned or that something suddenly came up and he would have to see me later. I bore everything quietly, even though I was deeply hurting inside. To find love after years of searching and then watch helplessly as you lose it so suddenly is something that nobody would like to experience.

Derrick and I were having problems in our relationship, but we were still together. In May 2016, about three weeks after the friendship breakup with Kay, Derrick and I were together when he went to take his bath, his mobile phone was on the table when a message came through. At first, I ignored it. But when another message came in, I decided to see who it was. On the lock screen, I saw the name Anika and read the messages. I knew his password. I unlocked his phone and went to his messages. There were messages from different women, all of which strongly suggested he was cheating on me. Most of the messages were from Anika and came with an outbreak of many lewd words. Derrick had been with loads of women even before our Vegas trip.

After reading through the messages, I dropped his phone where it was and waited until he was through taking his bath.

"Everything okay?" he asked when he entered the room.

The look on my face must have given the heaviness in my heart away. I learned something long before now: don't permit situations to determine your response. In this case, I didn't. I did as if nothing was wrong.

"Yea, I'm fine," I said, smiling at him. Whatever his excuses were for cheating on me and for going out with all those women, I was not having the emotional energy to hear them.

The whole "Baby momma" scenes followed this discovery quite early. One evening, I was with my son trying to read a book. He was playing with my phone when I heard the Facebook message beep. He rushed and gave it to me. I collected the phone and read the message:

"I'm still with Derrick! He's MINE!!!"

I sprang up on my feet when I read the message.

"Is everything okay, mom?" my son asked. I turned and looked at his face. It was filled with worry and concerns.

I patted his hair, reassuringly. "It's okay. It's nothing much. I just got a message I wasn't expecting. Go back and play."

My son had not taken a step when another message came up:

"This is a warning. Derrick is my man. Stay AWAY!!!

The messages didn't stop coming. For the next few days, I kept receiving them. And with each arrival, there was always something to reveal. For instance, a week after her first message, the messages that followed made it clear, should it be that I was still doubting, that she and Derrick were still quite together. Although it was an on-and-off relationship, there was no one, not even me, to break them apart. She and Derrick were meant to be together, forever. At some point, I began to think that the sender was Anika. But I wasn't sure. There were already too many other women in Derrick's life that I wasn't aware of.

I still didn't tell Derrick what was going on. But I noticed that his attitude towards me was beginning to change. He had always been a gentleman. There was something about his recent congeniality—it proved to me that he already knew I knew about his flirtations with various women. Most times, he couldn't even look me in the face. His shame was palpable, and I began to feel for him. On my end, I was careful– careful enough so that when things turned ugly, I would be able to save myself and my children.

And then I got pregnant and had an abortion immediately. When Derrick found out, he was so afraid and furious at the same time.

"They're gonna disown me if they find out," he told me.

I didn't know what to say. But I knew what to do. In 2018, I set morals aside and got pregnant again for him. My conviction is this: When he found out I did this just for his sake, he would see how loyal I was to him and that his happiness also mattered to me. I strongly believed it would keep him.

I was wrong. It didn't keep him. Or, at least, in the way I had thought it would. And that was another of the many lessons I came to learn:

You cannot keep anyone in your life who doesn't want to be kept. Many people are in your life because they want to be. They can wake up the next day and decide they're done. They need to be somewhere else and there's nothing you or anyone can do about that.

I tried to make sure that my days were normal even with the pregnancy. For the first two months, my life revolved around work, home, work, home, and nothing spectacular.

I put trust in God and accepted whatever was coming towards me. What had happened to me multiple times in my life was that

I could not always get everything I wanted out of life. I'd been there. Many times. And it was tough accepting that fact. I had to deal with several breakups, near-death, rape, relationship abuse, financial abuse, career problems.

When I realized my helplessness in the scheme of things happening to me, I would cry out to a power that I know would be higher than me– God! I would plead with Him to remember His promises to me, to make things better, to make meaning out of my life.

The things happening to me weren't part of the way I'd visualized my life. For the next few months, I was quietly waiting for the news that something big and better would happen for me. I was passing in between meditation, prayers, dwelling, and trusting in God to do his work.

Something did happen. But it was never in the way I'd expected.

In August 2016, one early Monday morning, I got a life-changing call. It was from my doctor's office. I had gone to do a test about a week ago and had almost forgotten about it.

His voice was sober on the phone as he spoke to me. When he finished speaking, I was quiet on my end.

"Hello, Torchia. Are you there?" he asked.

Silence.

I sniffed. "I am. Thank you, Dr. Ben."

After the call, I slumped into the nearest chair and wept my eyes out. Dr. Ben had just confirmed that I had an ailment that I was going to live with for the rest of my life.

That was the day I embraced the mirror. Each time I walked past it; I would stand before the mirror to take a long look at myself. What did I do to deserve this? Were my sins coming back to haunt me? Why did things keep getting this worse? I would spend the next few days asking questions that seemed to have no answers.

One of the greatest tragedies in life is that many people who genuinely need help have no one they trust enough to talk to about their deepest fears. I had no one. And my fears were mounting. That time, I wasn't thinking about my children, Derrick, or anyone else. I was thinking about myself.

I began to think of ways to put an end to my life. April came to my house before I could follow through with killing myself. I knew the Lord placed her in my life for a reason.

On the second morning of the day that I wanted to end it all, I began to rearrange my scattered room first. After taking a few things and changing their position in the room, I went to the table and saw my Bible. I took it from the table to drop it among my other books. I took two steps from the table and decided to open it for no reason.

I opened the pages of the Bible and as soon as I did that, my eyes fell on Esther 4:14–

"Perhaps you were born for such a time as this."

That part of the verse was highlighted. I could not remember doing that. However, I didn't read further again. The words took me by such force that I retreated to the edge of the bed and held the Bible in my hands, shaking.

I had been so caught up with the misfortunes of my life that I was beginning to forget God's promises to me, who was among those who are called to His purpose (Romans 8:28).

I was in this particular spot in my life because God wanted me to be here. My life may not have been going as I desired but I was now certain of one thing: God will surely have His way and accomplish all the promises He has for me. All He needed me to do was to surrender to His will.

Afterward, I read through the Bible, asked God for forgiveness, and prayed.

The waiting began.

CHAPTER 10

THE ARMS OF GOD

"His arms are forgiving"– Luke 15:20

I became pregnant with twins. Derrick and I were overjoyed. Derrick became so overtly attentive to me in a way that he had never been since we met. This went on for three months until we entered into the fourth month, and we were struck by another tragedy. I lost my babies.

The feeling of sadness was powerful and uncontrollable. Everything around me unsettled me as I continued to find it hard to come to terms with the fact that they were gone. I remember walking inside and around the house saying to myself repeatedly: "I want my babies back. I want my babies back." The ache to know them, to feel their kicks became almost unnatural. At night, after finally going to sleep, I would feel as if they were still kicking inside of me. Sometimes, I woke up suddenly as if the sound of my babies crying were calling me.

My mind was also running on short-term memory as I began to forget things quite easily. I experienced five miscarriages; I began to feel as if God had cursed me from the abortion, I had in 2016.

This went on for about a month until I finally embraced the strength that God gave me to carry on. I absorbed everything that had happened and accepted, once again, God's hand in the scheme of things.

Two months after I lost my babies, I found out that Derrick got his Baby Momma pregnant. It was at this point that I felt my whole world crumbling down again, just when I'd thought I was recovering.

It was his betrayal and inconsideration that messed me up.

While I was fighting for my girls' life in February, he was out there doing his own thing, finding ways to gratify his desires. For the next few years (2018-2020), our relationship was greatly battered. We were on and off.

Sometimes it seemed as if we would never be together again. But it wasn't so. Although things were happening, we couldn't stay apart from each other. I saw greatness in Derrick, and I never cared about what the outer side of him portrayed. I was convinced he was a great guy and that he was not a completely bad person.

As tough as my life had been, I had been making sure for years to learn how to practice forgiveness and give the people I loved a second chance. All I would ask from God would be the grace to know when to let go, and the strength to do so.

In 2018, I gained 50 pounds. I could no longer fit into my favorite jeans, even buttoning them was a struggle for me. When I looked in the mirror at my brown chestnut complexion body, it seemed as if someone was about to take over my body from me and there was nothing that I or anyone could do about it.

It was also obvious that the people around me were also noticing the changes in me. I've always been aware that most of the comments about weight could usually puncture the heart without mercy, especially when they come from people who have always judged you by your physical appearance. I began to struggle with my weight and hated how I was looking. Gradually, the fear for my mental health crept in.

I sat down one day and reviewed my life in the past few months. Afterward, I made a promise to myself: Before the year ran out, I would be putting myself in therapy.

It was a promise I kept.

In the first week of December, I began therapy. I wanted to find help that would be mentally, physically, and emotionally sustaining for long term. I have been in therapy ever since. It has been helpful for me from day one, and I was able to maintain good mental health and to make sure that my thought patterns are always positive.

*   *   *   *

If one begins to go through the Bible, it wouldn't take long for them to discover that God usually works in secret. In a quiet voice and way of doing things that are so different from the ways of men, God has continued to bless and uplift those who believe in him. While we may not think of stunning miracles, massive revelations, or visions of God, accepting that working in the secret is God's nature.

All I needed to do to partake in these secret works that God is doing on behalf of his children is to believe. I can be strengthened enough to hold on to this faith through the Spirit of God which is in me (Ephesians 3:16).

*   *   *   *

In 2019, a few months after I began therapy, I got a big break that set in to stabilize my financial standing. God was blessing me, and I was opening myself unto him with gratitude. I had no faintest doubt that after all those years that I came to accept God's promises, it was time for Him to rise for me. Everywhere I turned to, there was this feeling, this voice, and these soft words telling me that I should let God do His thing; it's time.

In the middle of the year, from the help of public housing, I and my children moved into an 1800 sq ft home. Once this was done, I was able to save and get back on track.

Finally, I did something that felt as if it was coming at the appointed time. I began to follow the instructions from Habakkuk 2:2–

> *"And the LORD answered me: "Write the vision; make it plain on tablets, so he may run who reads it."*

I wrote down goals to write a book, save, and get a job. I did all of these things and watched as God brought everything to light in March 2021.

*   *   *   *

How do we discover wholeness? How do we share our pain, hurt, and disappointment with those around us? How do we, as friends share hope with loved ones who are chained, deeply hurt, and separated from the freedom God wants us to enjoy?

Express the pain. Cry if you so much desire. Don't be ashamed of releasing out all those bad vibes and hurt.

By accepting that abuse is not welcomed and runs completely counter to God and his ways. God seeks healing, well-being, and prosperity for his people.

We should never falter to keep the truth straight. One golden principle that has been reversed and twisted to suit human needs and interests is the Bible Scripture found in Ephesians 5:21

"Submit to one another out of reverence for Christ."

Abusive people try to use God's Word to manipulate, blame, accuse and get their way. We forget that God expects a dual commitment of love from both men and women in a healthy relationship.

However, for many of us who have experienced God's perfect love, we are aware that submission is mutual and rooted in love for one another.

Self-sacrifice for the good of your spouse and family should be the vanguard of all you do. Wives too should choose to love, showing respect, support, and honor instead of seeking to control, coerce, dominate, or force.

Allow yourself to recover from the pain so the pain is no longer buried deep inside.

*   *   *   *

Derrick and I began our journey walking with God. We did this separately. Our intention was for each of us to experience God individually, know His core plans for our lives, before facing each other as a couple.

After Derrick and I continued to live in sin, God delivered us, and we decided to enter into a holy marriage. We did that on Sunday, May 30th, 2021.

This is my life today. God has brought me to a place of balance and abundance. Despite all that happened to me, despite all the foul and explicit scandals that accompanied me from childhood to my adulthood, there are still things today that I wished I had learned earlier when I was much younger.

But it doesn't matter. I have given myself to Christ. In Him, and the strength of His forgiven arms, I am a different person today than I had been years ago. It's okay that I've lost friends along the way. The way that I walk, and talk is totally different. I am free, and the moral of my story is that: sometimes God will send and use us in the lives of others to bring them out of the wilderness. Sacrificing ourselves so that God's glory prevails is called being and walking in obedience. Derrick and I overcame adversity and kept the faith, now we get the opportunity to live abundantly together by the grace of God.

I embrace heaven and earth with gratitude. It is all I can do right now. Rejoice with me for the new things in my life.

EPILOGUE

A FEW THINGS TO NOTE

"God will be with you on your sleepless nights, and will dry your tears with His love. God is for the valiant." Paulo Coelho, *Maktub*

This is it, my story in your hands. I feel excited and so free inside to know that you have read up to this point. What more can I ask than to say "Thank you" for going on this journey with me? THANK YOU!!!

As I write this last part of my book, drawing it to its inevitable conclusion, I am deliberate about letting my son distract me. I am taking short pauses to steal little glances at him and his little sister. He's heading to college anytime soon. They know my story, these wonderful children of mine. And I have so much trust in God that they will use my story to guide them in life.

I grew up and was thrown into the world without a survival guide. I had accidents, passed through the storms, got broken, abandon, abused, betrayed, lost friendships and everything negative came my way. But I was never alone in the whole universe. God was watching over me, waiting for the right time to bless me. And He kept His promises when they were due.

My son says something to my daughter, and she laughs heartedly before she drives him away from her sight. He shakes his head mockingly and then disappears from her sight.

She raises her head and sees me looking at her.

"Mom!" she calls out. "What are you looking at?"

I must have been looking at her for a long time for her to notice.

"You," I confess.

She laughs again. My daughter has rich, sincere, and intense laughter. Whenever she laughs, she throws her head back, and then a fascinating look comes into her eyes. At first, a smile will tug at her lips before breaking into a grin, and then a burst of wide laughter. All of this happen within seconds. As I think about her laughter, I realize that her brother also has the same beautiful laughter.

"Why?" she asks when she is finally in control of her breath.

"You're very beautiful," I say. I can see the semblance of satisfaction settling on her face. I go for the kill: "I love beautiful things. I love looking at them. And now, I have you and your brother to look at as long as I am alive."

My words are both a mixture of compliments to her beauty and gratitude to God for giving me everything that I have today.

My daughter walks up to me and embraces me. We hold each other as if our lives depend on it.

Someone chuckles. I raise my heart and see my son standing by the door.

"Come here handsome," I say. He does and melts into our embrace.

I have been writing and reading and doing a lot of work these past few days. Hugging my children right now feels like I am revitalizing all my weak spots.

I feel happy these past few years more than I had ever been in my entire life. Born on the South Side of Chicago, I came from nothing. I went from city to city, shelter to shelter begging for acceptance. I spent years feeling all alone in the world. My search for acceptance leaded me into the arms of the wrong people. My memories were shattered, my childhood was stolen before I could understand it, and my adulthood pitched in darkness for years before God came for me.

Things are okay for me now. As you have read this book to this final stage, I hope my story has taught you something. If you're passing through what I passed through, you could take note of the few things below, and I pray to God almighty that they are of further help to you.

Embrace God's presence

Soaking in God's presence and truth has a way of liberating your soul in ways like never before. God is in the business of mind renewable. His word says, 'there are new every morning. Great is thy faithfulness.' Spending time with God through acts of Word study, prayer, worship, and fellowship has a way of opening up your heart to the goodness and richness of God and earth. You might be broken but gradually you will get to that point where you become an overcomer.

Seek support and set loving boundaries

Saying NO is not ungodly. No one should make you feel inferior or abandoned. Set limits and stick to them. Setting limits can be difficult but necessary. Demand the abuser to go get help. In today's world, there's a lot of pressure to forgive an abuser coming from family (especially when the abuser is a relative), friends, relatives, and church members. You hear, "Oh you need to forgive him so you can move on." 'You should be over this by now, why are you still stuck on living in the past?" 'Jesus would want you to reconcile you know.' This is coming from a well of concern, but forgiveness is not a feeling. Forgiveness is not saying, "I forgive you when your abuser says sorry, sometimes, the abuser tenders no apologies, yet we carelessly place the burden of forgiving so quickly on the slacken shoulders of victims. The need for abusers to confess, repent, and respect boundaries set by the victim is not so strong when compared to the clamor for the victim to just forgive and forget.

Begin the Journey with forgiveness

Forgiveness is accepting the reality of what has happened. It is going beyond the point of anger and consumption in fear and frustration. Coming from a place of forgiveness, you can as a victim put your thoughts out there and thrive without dwelling on the abuser but healing. Always remember forgiveness is not a phrase, 'I forgive you but a journey to self that can't be summed up in a single moment of time or sentence.

Forgiveness is a choice and process that doesn't equal reconciliation. An abused woman has to be transformed from within by the experience that results in her letting go of anger and frustration and ultimately being able to think more of the offender without boiling up again.

It is crucial to know that one who is truly remorseful for what they've done to you will respect your right of choice. They won't hold it against you that you are yet to forgive them neither will they compel your behavior and relations towards them in the future. They will accept the boundaries you set willingly and the repercussions for their actions. They won't pressure you into forgiving them when you're not yet ready and they won't expect reconciliation with them simply because you've forgiven them.

Due to the nature of human dynamics, there has never been a one-size-fits-all prescription for forgiveness and healing, but it is important to assess your situation. Tell yourself the truth, as well much as it hurts and tastes bitter. Denial is one of the most hallmarks of abuse and total healing won't come from living in a state of denial.

119

Admit you are being abused, recognize the damage that has been done and invite the Holy Spirit to reveal the reality of the situation to you and help you overcome it.

Remember that, forgiveness is a choice, not a feeling. Forgive yourself and the abuser. God will deal with them. Tap into God's redemptive purpose for your life and sooner or later, you will be a channel of healing to others.

Separate physically from your partner so they know you won't continue living the same way.

This can help protect you and your children. Separating can also be a mutual agreement for you both to work on your problems to reconcile. It can be tough, but the gravity of the situation will require you to run for safety.

Seek professional help and guidance.

The healing process is a lengthy and difficult voyage full of emotional landmines and you will need professional help to walk through potentially explosive and destructive situations. You'll need to develop a strategy for change. Healthy social connections contribute to better overall health, so it is critical to explore support from family, friends, and church.

Decisions about your safety and the safety of your kids or any child under your care are usually difficult. There are a lot of risks to be considered both physical and emotional harm, the safety of children, family, and friends, access to financial resources, religious beliefs, the loss of the relationship, and risks involving arrest, detention, or even immigration status. Additional life challenges such as lack of affordable housing, physical or mental disability, or lack of immigration status may stare you hard in the face.

Regaining and maintaining control over your thoughts, decisions, and actions

Everything about your life can help in no small measure to rebuild confidence and your sense of power and freedom from the domination and violence of an abuser.

Hope is the life force that you should hold onto for it will surely keep you going. No matter how bad it gets, you as a person are more knowledgeable about yourself. You're better equipped to evaluate the risks that may come with staying or leaving an abusive relationship.

While there's no way to anticipate whether your abusive partner's behavior will continue to hurt you and your children, there are warning signs that you should watch out for such as a history of domestic violence including sex, attempted strangulation, or physical abuse during pregnancy. Threats to kill you and your children or family members or friends is another red light, threats of suicide by the abuser 'If you leave me, I'm going to kill myself and it will be on your hands' is another way an abuser manipulates you, the abuser also becomes obsessive, controlling, and coercive in behavior going as far as monitoring every single thing you do, extreme possessiveness and stalking. Maybe before now, you had already contacted the police for help or assistance for domestic violence or other criminal behavior. The abuser's consumption of alcohol and drug abuse also spikes up. A combination of these conditions increases the likelihood of death. Even the absence of these factors shouldn't make you sigh for relief as you are still not safe. If you feel worried about your safety, speak to someone - the police department, a close family, or a friend for assistance. Also, talking to an attorney could be of help.

If you have time, start putting aside cash

Preferably somewhere other than your house. Leave clothes, important items, and documents with a friend in case you have to leave quickly. Memorize phone numbers of close friends or places you could call for help. It's possible that you might be leaving quickly so keep the change (for a payphone). You could also create a code word with family, friends, and colleagues so that you can tell them to call for help without alerting the abuser. After leaving, change your phone number immediately but if you stay, change the locks on your house. Always have a close ally sleepover. Alter your routines frequently and if you have to meet the abuser, do so in a public places.

Protecting your kids sometimes means letting them know what's up.

Any form of violence hurts children's sense of safety and security. It is important to help them know what they should instead be thinking about. If you have to go out, make sure to tell them where and when you will be back, make sure they sleep enough, exercise, and eat healthy foods. Understand how important you are in your children's lives. Try every day to protect them. Emotionally be connected to them even as you are firm, loving, and understanding. Listen to know their needs. Having an emotional support system and staying connected to them can also go a long way in the healing process. You could try school things, faith-based activities, arts, sports, club activities, after-

school programs that can be beneficial. It is easier to find counseling or support groups when participating in such activities. Another crucial point is to stay in touch with your family and friends.

Take care of yourself. Don't let your abuser steal you from yourself. I know that this is hard to do. But you can do it. I believe in you. Your physical, emotional, mental, and spiritual health is just as important, especially to your children. When you care well for yourself, you possess the energy to not only look after your children but to truly enjoy them and be there for them. You are bound to do better in life if you feel good about yourself. Build skills, focus on what you're doing well, appreciate your efforts, reward yourself instead of name-calling, shaming, or guilt-tripping every time something goes wrong. Practice daily self-care routines, be kind and compassionate to yourself. Breathe. Slowly. Drink water to keep you hydrated throughout the day, take a few minutes each day and do something restorative that you love. It could be drinking coffee at your favorite restaurant or spot, having quiet moments to reflect and think positive thoughts, short walks, dance, just spending time with family and friends, or bathing in the sun.

Healing will give you a new purpose to life and embolden you to get more involved in your community by expressing your experiences through art, photography or dance will help you in sharing your stories with those who are struggling. You can also become an advocate for gender equity.

Thank you for reading my story!!